QUEEN & COUNTRY™

GREG RUCKA

QUEEN & COUNTRY™

WRITTEN BY
GREG RUCKA

ILLUSTRATED BY
STEVE ROLSTON, BRIAN HURTT, LEANDRO FERNANDEZ, CHRISTINE NORRIE, BRYAN LEE O'MALLEY, & STAN SAKAI

LETTERING BY
SEAN KONOT & JOHN DRANSKI

COVER BY
TIM SALE

BOOK DESIGN BY
KEITH WOOD

COLLECTION EDITED BY
JAMES LUCAS JONES

ORIGINAL SERIES EDITED BY
JAMIE S. RICH & JAMES LUCAS JONES

Published by Oni Press, Inc.
Joe Nozemack, publisher
James Lucas Jones, editor in chief
Randal C. Jarrell, managing editor

This collects issues 1-12 of the Oni Press comics series *Queen & Country* as well as material from the *Oni Press Color Special* 2001.

ONI PRESS, INC.
1305 SE Martin Luther King Jr. Blvd.
Suite A
Portland, OR 97214
USA

www.onipress.com

First edition: December 2007
ISBN-13: 978-1-932664-87-4
ISBN-10: 1-929998-87-4

1 3 5 7 9 10 8 6 4 2

PRINTED IN CANADA.

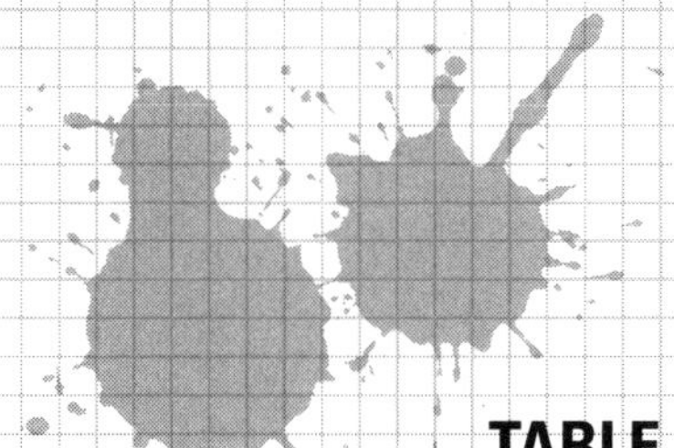

TABLE OF CONTENTS

OPERATION: BROKEN GROUND 1

OPERATION: MORNINGSTAR 119

OPERATION: CRYSTAL BALL 201

BEHIND THE SCENES 331

ABOUT THE AUTHORS 357

OPERATION: BROKEN GROUND

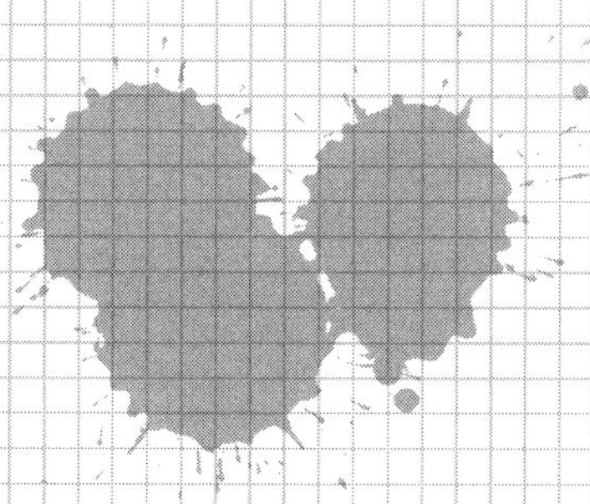

WRITTEN BY
GREG RUCKA

ILLUSTRATED BY
STEVE ROLSTON

LETTERED BY
SEAN KONOT

INTERLUDE ILLUSTRATED & LETTERED BY
STAN SAKAI

WITH TONES BY
TOM LUTH

ORIGINALLY EDITIED BY
JAMIE S. RICH

ROSTER

C—Ubiquitous code-name for the current head of S.I.S.. Real name is Sir Wilson Stanton Davies.

DONALD WELDON—Deputy Chief of Service, has oversight of all aspects of Intelligence gathering and operations. Immediate superior to Crocker.

PAUL CROCKER—Director of Operations, encompassing all field work in all theaters of operations. In addition to commanding individual stations, has direct command of the Special Section–sometimes referred to as Minders –used for special operations.

TOM WALLACE—Head of the Special Section, a Special Operations Officer with the designation Minder One Responsible for the training and continued well-being of his unit, both at home and in the field. Six year veteran of the Minders.

TARA CHACE—Special Operations Officer, designated Minder Two. Entering her third year as Minder.

EDWARD KITTERING—Special Operations Officer, designated Minder Three. Has been with the Special Section for less than a year.

OPS ROOM STAFF

OTHERS

ALEXIS—Mission Control Officer (also called Main Communications Officer)– responsible for maintaining communications between the Operations Room and the agents in the field.

RON—Duty Operations Officer, responsible for monitoring the status and importance of all incoming intelligence, both from foreign stations and other sources.

KATE—Personal Assistant to Paul Crocker, termed P.A. to D.Ops. Possibly the hardest and most important job in the Service.

ANGELA CHANG—CIA Station Chief in London. Has an unofficial intelligence-sharing arrangement with Crocker.

SIMON RAYBURN—Director of Intelligence for S.I.S. (D. Int), essentially Crocker's opposite number. Responsible for the evaluation, interpretation, and dissemination of all acquired intelligence.

DAVID KINNY—Crocker's opposite number at M.I.5, also called the Security Services, with jurisdiction primarily confined to within the U.K.

CHAPTER 1

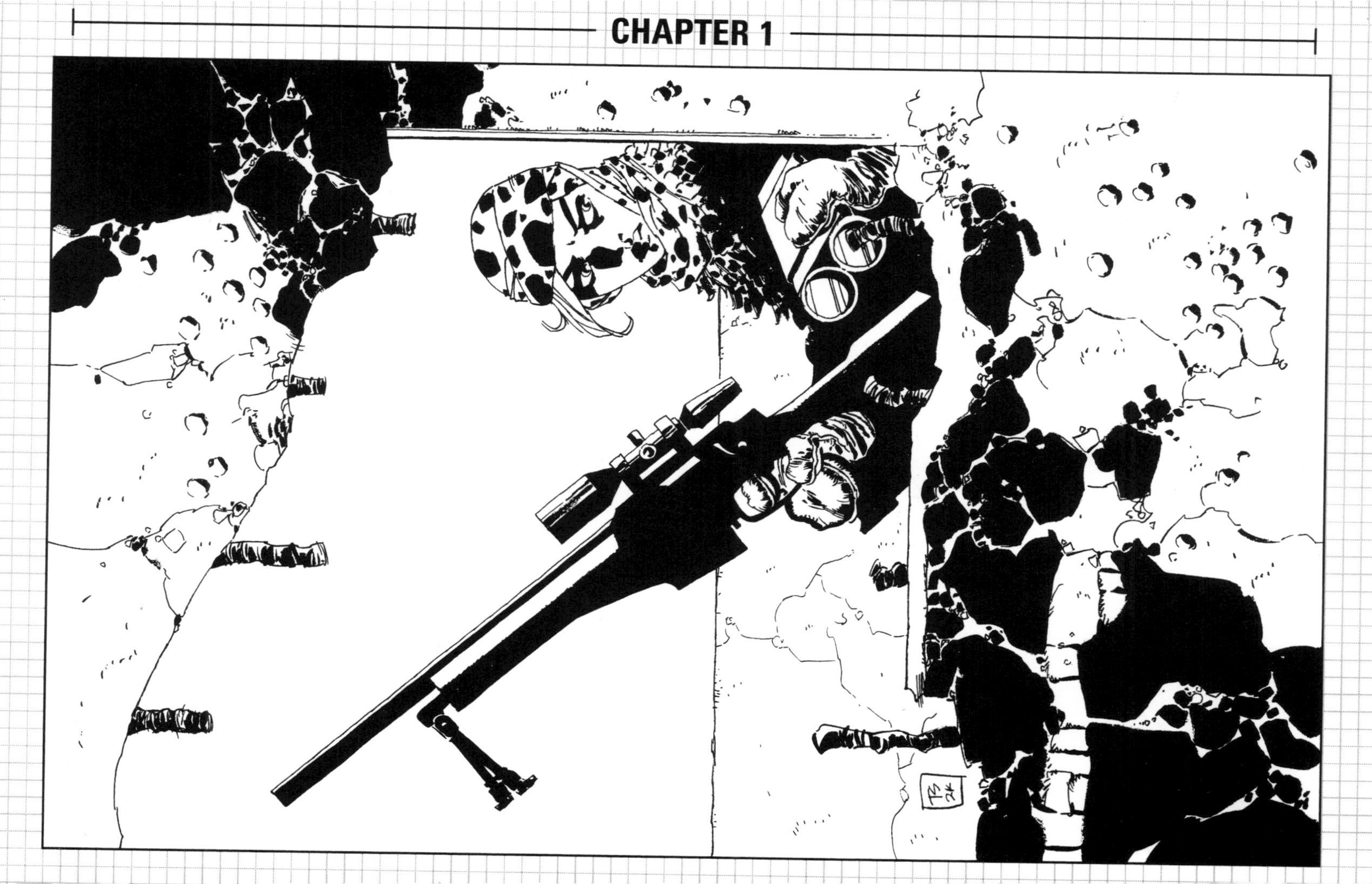

... STANDING BY...
CAN WE REACH HER?
YES, SIR. SHE'S ON A *SHORT LEAD*, VIA THE ISTANBUL NUMBER TWO. CALL SIGN *RAVEN*.
HE'S ON A SAT-LINK TO HER. CALL SIGN *CROW*. SHE'S IN POSITION...
0504 (z)
KOSOVO
... BEEN THERE ALL NIGHT.
MUST BE BLOODY *FREEZING*.
YES, SIR.
-- ENTERING PRIZREN NOW.
0504 (z)
NOVI PAZAI
MITROVICA
PRISTINA
OPERATION: BROKEN GROUND
STATUS: HOLDING
PRIZREN
SKOPJE
KOSOVO
LEX, WHEN'S *SUNRISE* IN *ZONE?*

OH-FIVE-SEVENTEEN, SIR.
ARE WE ABORTING?
PAUL?
SUNLIGHT HITS HER POSITION, SHE'LL BE BLOWN.
SHE'LL BE BLOWN AS SOON AS SHE PULLS THE TRIGGER.
THE QUESTION IS, CAN SHE GET OUT IN TIME?
THE QUESTION IS, CAN SHE HIT THE TARGET?
YOU KNOW SHE CAN, BOSS...
... IT'S WHY YOU SENT HER AND NOT ME.
WHAT'S MARKOVSKY'S ETA?
CHECKING, SIR...
WELL...?! HURRY IT UP!
0507 (z)
OPERATION: BROKEN GROUND
STATUS: HOLDING
KOSOV

SIR? RAVEN IS ASKING FOR INSTRUCTIONS.
TELL HIM TO BLOODY WELL WAIT! IT'S NOT HIS ASS IN THE NEST, IS IT?!
SHE GETS CAUGHT, THE FOREIGN OFFICE'LL EAT ME FOR DINNER.
DON'T TELL ME YOU DIDN'T CLEAR THE RUN?!
I COULDN'T RISK WELDON SAYING NO.
IT'S CONFIRMED, SIR. MARKOVSKY CAME IN OVER THE MACEDONIA BORDER TWENTY-THREE MINUTES AGO, THROUGH THE GERMAN SECTOR.
WELL, THAT'S THAT, THEN, ISN'T IT?
LEX, ORDER TO RAVEN FROM D. OPS...
... TELL HIM CROW IS FREE TO FLY.
YES, SIR.
M.C.O. FOR RAVEN, ORDERS AS FOLLOWS:
FROM DIRECTOR OPERATIONS PAUL CROCKER...
MITROVICA
PRIST
OPERATION: BROKEN GROUND
STATUS: FREE RUN
PRIZREN
KOS

"... CROW IS FREE TO FLY."
The last time I was this cold, I was at the South Pole.
Why doesn't Crocker ever send me somewhere hot?
Need to compensate for the wind...
... maybe he won't show...

Dammit...
... get out of the truck, General.
Inspect the merchandise. Do something...
... give me a shot.
There you go, they've bought the guns, now give the nice soldiers their money...
Good... good...
... inhale...
... exhale...
... hold...
... and...

U.N.

UN

And it was going so well...

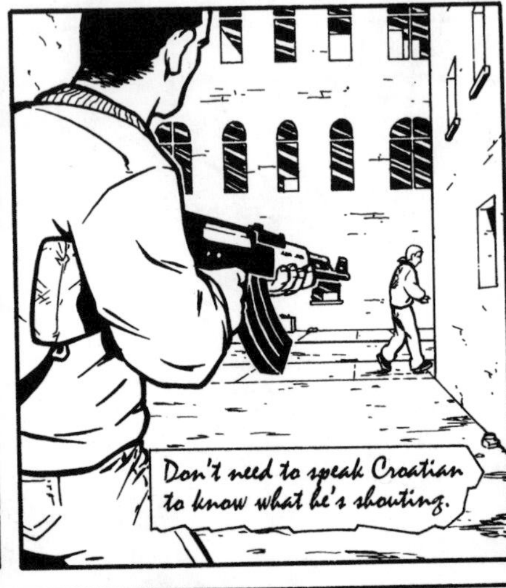
Don't need to speak Croatian to know what he's shouting.

What is it Wallace always says?

It's not the bullet that has your name on it you have to worry about...

... it's all those other ones...

... marked "To whom it may concern."
U.N.

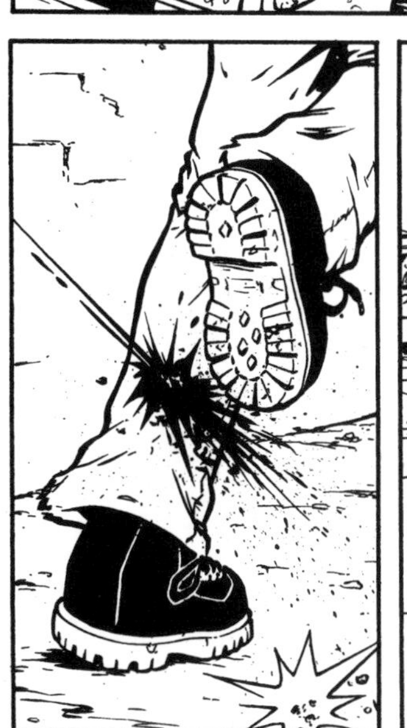

... bloody hell...

... I don't want to die in Kosovo.

SIR? JUST IN FROM PRIZREN...

... REPORTS OF GUNFIRE AND A PURSUIT.
ANYTHING ELSE?
YES, SIR. ONE FATALITY, MALE.

SO SHE GOT HIM BEFORE SHE WAS BLOWN.
IS THAT GOING TO HELP YOU SLEEP BETTER WHEN SHE DOESN'T COME BACK?

LEX, WHAT'S THE EGRESS?
ISTANBUL NUMBER TWO RECRUITED DRIVER PICKS HER UP NORTH OF PRIZREN. TRAVEL VIA U.N. VEHICLE, U.N. COVER NORTH TO PRISTINA...

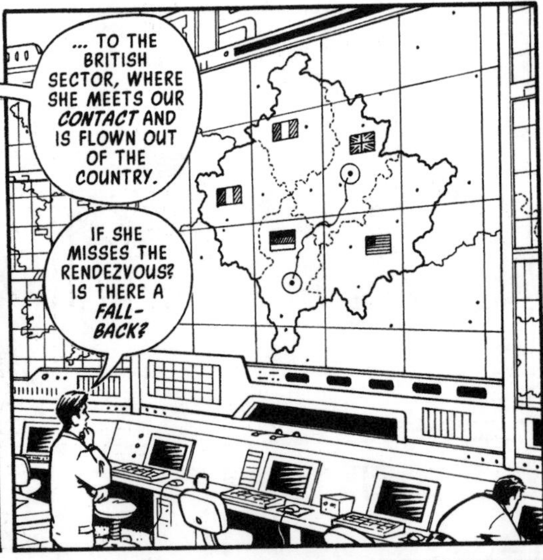
... TO THE BRITISH SECTOR, WHERE SHE MEETS OUR CONTACT AND IS FLOWN OUT OF THE COUNTRY.
IF SHE MISSES THE RENDEZVOUS? IS THERE A FALL-BACK?

NO, SIR. SHE'S ON HER OWN.

AND UNARMED?
YES. SHE WAS TO GO WEAPONLESS AFTER THE HIT, IN CASE SHE WAS STOPPED AT ANY OF THE CHECKPOINTS...

EIGHTY-SEVEN KILOMETERS FROM *PRIZREN* TO *PRISTINA.*
WITH *K.L.A., NATO,* AND *U.N.* TROOPS ALL ALONG THE WAY.
DUTY OPS OFFICER...

YES, SIR. I'LL TELL HIM...
YOU GOING TO NOTIFY THE FOREIGN OFFICE?
NOT *YET.* SHE *COULD* STILL MAKE IT.

DEPUTY CHIEF, SIR. WANTS TO SEE YOU IN HIS OFFICE RIGHT AWAY.

CALL ME IF THERE ARE ANY DEVELOPMENTS.
WHAT'RE YOU GOING TO TELL WELDON?

DEPENDS ON HOW MUCH HE *ALREADY KNOWS.*

First rule...
... keep moving.
Second rule...
... find a crowd.

U.N.

PAUL, I HOPE I DIDN'T DISTURB YOU?
I WAS IN THE OPS ROOM.
YES, I KNOW.
WHAT I DON'T KNOW IS WHY TARA CHACE IS IN KOSOVO.
IS SHE?
YOU DAMN WELL KNOW SHE IS!
YOU'RE RUNNING A SPECIAL OPERATION IN KOSOVO AND I WANT TO KNOW WHY!
WHAT THE HELL IS BROKEN GROUND?!
I WANT AN ANSWER, PAUL.
IT'S A FAVOR TO THE C.I.A.-- FORMER RUSSIAN GENERAL IGOR GRIGORIVICH MARKOVSKY.
HE'S RETIRED, MARKOVSKY.
HE'S RUSSIAN MOB, BUYING GUNS FROM THE K.L.A. AND THEN SELLING THEM TO THE CHECHENS.

C.I.A. ASKED IF WE COULD PUT A STOP TO IT.

YOU USED ONE OF HER MAJESTY'S AGENTS TO COMMIT MURDER AT THE AMERICANS' BEHEST?

NOT FOR FREE.
IN EXCHANGE, WE GET KEY-HOLE SUPPORT AND ANALYSIS FOR OUR OPERATIONS IN NORTH AFRICA AND ASIA.

THAT'S INTELLIGENCE WE COULDN'T GET OTHERWISE.
THAT HARDLY JUSTIFIES YOU MOUNTING AN UNAUTHORIZED ASSASSINATION!

I THINK IT DOES. THE C.I.A. DOES FAVORS FOR US ALL THE TIME.
NOW THEY OWE ME.
YOU?!

US.
NOW THEY OWE US. IT'S GOOD FOR THE SERVICE, SIR.

I HOPE THAT'LL BE CONSOLATION FOR CHACE'S FAMILY.

I DOUBT IT, SIR...

... SHE DOESN'T HAVE ANY.

Blown the rendezvous to hell.
UN

Crocker must be apoplectic.

Weldon's got to know by now, too.
Wonder who won that fight.

Lucky it was only a ricochet that hit me.

Hurts like hell all the same.

Time to go.

Too much hope that the keys are in.

At least the door's unlocked.

Old-fashioned ignition. Good...

... just need a few seconds...

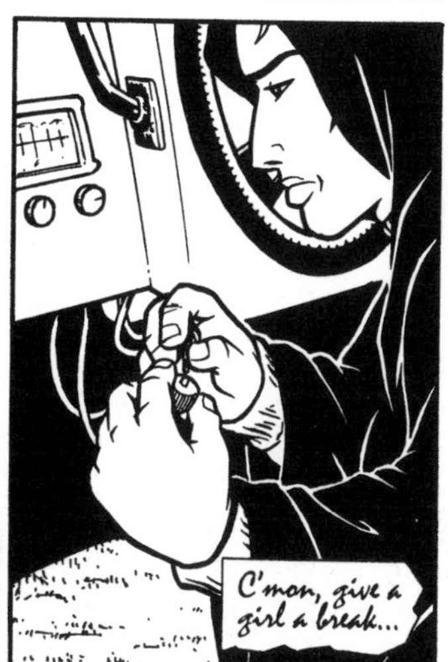
C'mon, give a girl a break...

... C'mon, start...

... Thank you...

PRISHTINE
62 km

Now we learn if that bloke got the license on this thing or not.

⟨WHERE ARE YOU HEADING?⟩
⟨PRISTINA.⟩

⟨YOU HAVE YOUR *PASS*?⟩
⟨HERE.⟩

⟨WHAT'S THIS?⟩

⟨OH... uh... NOTHING... IT'S *NOTHING.*⟩
⟨CAN I JUST HAVE THAT *BACK*?⟩

⟨ONE MOMENT, PLEASE.⟩

That's right, that's it, ignore the pass...
... It's a forgery, after all...
... And don't pay any attention to the blood on my pant leg...
... just look at the picture, that's fine.
<EVERYTHING APPEARS FINE. HAVE A SAFE TRIP.>
<MAY I HAVE MY... um...>
<OH! YES, OF COURSE... SORRY... THE PICTURE IS OF *YOU*?>
<IT'S FOR MY BOYFRIEND...>
<OF COURSE, OF COURSE...>
<... DRIVE CAREFULLY.>
<THANK YOU.>

SERGEANT RAMSEY...?

... MY NAME'S CHACE. TARA CHACE.

I WAS GETTING *WORRIED* ABOUT YOU, MISS CHACE. YOU WERE SUPPOSED TO BE HERE *HOURS AGO.*

THERE WAS *TRAFFIC* ON THE *ROAD.*

GOOD LORD! ARE YOU *ALL RIGHT?!* YOU WANT A *MEDIC* TO TAKE A LOOK AT THAT?

IF IT'S NOT TOO MUCH *BOTHER.*

NOT AT *ALL.* I'LL BE *RIGHT BACK.*
TAKE YOUR *TIME...*

... TAKE YOUR TIME...

BOSS?
WHAT DO YOU *WANT*, TOM?

SIGNAL FROM ISTANBUL STATION.
CROW IS ON HER WAY HOME.

IS SHE ALL RIGHT?
SHE GOT *CLIPPED* IN THE LEG, BUT IT WASN'T *SERIOUS*.

GOOD.
I'LL WANT HER *REPORT* ON MY DESK *TOMORROW*.

WAS THERE SOME-THING ELSE?
NO, SIR.
THEN *SHOVE OFF*, TOM. I'VE GOT *WORK* TO DO.

THAT'S MY GIRL.

INTERLUDE

KOSOVO.
FIVE DAYS AGO.

1

ODESSA.
FOUR DAYS AGO.
<DIDN'T GO DOWN.>
<WHAT THE HELL-->
WHUMP!

<THERE WAS A SNIPER.>
<THE GENERAL'S HEAD POPPED LIKE A GRAPE.>
VODKA

<WHO?>

<I DON'T KNOW. I NEVER GOT A LOOK AT THE SHOOTER.>

<FIND OUT.>

SOFIA.
THREE DAYS AGO.
<...SAY IT WAS A **WOMAN?**>

<WOMAN, **YES**. WITH THE **BLOND** HAIR. PALE.>
<YOU THINK **AMERICAN?**>
<COULD **BE** AMERICAN, **YES.**>

<**OH!** AND SHE WAS **SHOT,** YES?>
<SHOT?>
<IN **LEG**. RIGHT LEG, I THINK.>

<COME **HERE.**>
<**SHOW** ME WHICH WAY SHE **RAN...**>
ITALIAN
FRENCH
BRITISH
AMERICAN

SKOPJE.
TWO DAYS AGO.
<...ERICH INSIDE, HE HAS A *GIRL* THERE.>
<YOU'RE *SURE* HE SAW HER?>

<HELL YEAH! SHE HAD A *NAKED* PICTURE OF HERSELF. HE WOULDN'T STOP *TALKING* ABOUT IT.>
<IT WAS *AFTER*, YOU KNOW, WHEN WE HEARD ABOUT THE *SHOOTING*.>

<THANKS.>

4

SOFIA.
YESTERDAY.
<...AWAKE NOW? GOOD.>
<LET'S TRY AGAIN.>

<LOOK AT THE PICTURES.>
<TELL US IF YOU SEE HER.>
<...PLEASE, I DON'T-->

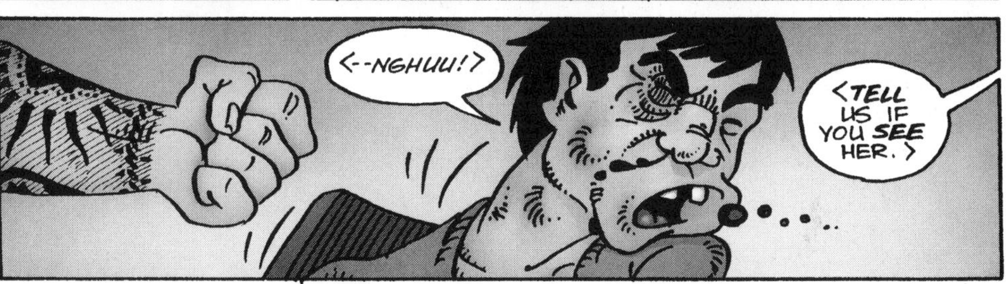
<--NGHUU!>
<TELL US IF YOU SEE HER.>

BRADY,
SHARI

GRIFFIN,
MAGGIE

KRINGLE,
CLAUDIA

PENTA,
DARIA

<...PLEASE...>
SCHUMAN,
IRENA

ODESSA.
THIS MORNING.
<THAT'S HER.>

<I GOT THE FILE FROM ONE OF OUR FRIENDS AT THE FSB.>
<SHE'S BRITISH INTELLIGENCE...>

<... PART OF THEIR OPERATIONS DIRECTORATE.>
<MULTIPLE WORK NAMES-- HENDERSON, NAYLOR, ROBINSON... GOES ON AND ON.>

<REAL NAME APPEARS TO BE CHACE, TARA FELICITY.>

<TELL OUR PEOPLE.>
<I WANT THE BRITISH HURT.>
<I WANT THAT BITCH DEAD.>

<ONE MILLION DOLLARS TO THE MAN WHO BRINGS ME HER HEAD.>
6.

CHAPTER 2

KEY
TARA'S VACANT LIST
MOVE CAR
CLEAN FRIDGE
DO LAUNDRY
WRITE EULOGY
SCHEDULE RANGETIME TO ZERO WEAPON
GRAIN PROD
U.K. PASSPORT
TS 01

LONDON.
ОСТОРОЖНОСТЬ

... THEN SHOUTING AT THE *RUSSIAN* DESK.
AND WHAT DID HIS *EMINENCE* D. OPS WANT?
TRYING TO TRACK TRANSFERS FROM ST. PETERSBURG TO LONDON MARITIME BANK OR SOME SUCH.
THOUGH WHY THIS HAS *CROCKER'S* KNICKERS IN A *TWIST* I'VE NO *CLUE.*
WELL, HE'S PLANNING A *SPECIAL OP* MOST LIKE, ISN'T HE?
UNDOUBTEDLY.
WHO KNOWS? MAYBE HE'LL EVEN GET *PERMISSION* FIRST.
〈FUCK WITH *US*...〉
〈... WE FUCK YOU *BACK.*〉

YOU MEAN THE WAY HE CLEARED CHACE'S RUN IN KOSOVO?
COULD DO. I HEAR THEY'RE FORECASTING *SNOW* IN *HELL* LATER TODAY, AS WELL.
WE'RE GOING TO BE AT THIS *ALL* NIGHT.
WITH *THAT* IN MIND, YOU WANT A COFFEE?
YOU'D BE SAVING MY *LIFE,* JILL...

BRRT
BRRT

BRRT--
3:51
CHACE.

DUTY OPS OFFICER. FROM D. OPS, MINDERS TO THE OPS ROOM.
TEN MINUTES.

OH DAMN.

OH, DAMN...

MOVE THE VEHICLE, PLEASE...
... YOU CAN'T PARK HERE.

YES, I CAN.

JESUS.

TARA!

WHAT THE HELL HAPPENED?
YOU'RE HEAD OF SECTION. *YOU* TELL *ME*.

I'M SUPPOSED TO STILL BE ON *DISABILITY*.
THERE IS NO DISABILITY WHEN CROCKER *SCRAMBLES* THE SECTION.

HOW *ARE* YOU FEELING?
LEG'S FINE, TOM.

THEY'RE *BOTH* FINE, YOU ASK *ME*, BUT THAT'S *NOT* WHAT I MEANT.
I KNOW WHAT YOU *MEANT*.

... ROTATING THE SURVEILLANCE...
... THE M.O.D. ABOUT SHORT-RANGE ROCKETS...
... AT THE HOME OFFICE, SENDING SOMEONE FROM FIVE...
WHERE THE HELL HAVE YOU TWO BEEN?
THE HONEYMOON WAS SHORT BUT SWEET.
MORNING, ED.
HEY, TOM.
TARA. HOW'S YOUR LEG?
IT WORKS.
SIR.
SIT DOWN, TARA.

AT SIX MINUTES BEFORE FOUR THIS MORNING, THE FIFTH FLOOR WAS HIT BY A ROCKET ATTACK.
RIGHT NOW WE DON'T KNOW WHO, WHAT, OR WHY.

INTEL IS ON WITH THE M.O.D., TRYING TO DETERMINE THE NATURE OF THE WEAPON, AND THE POLICE HAVE STARTED A CANVASS.

HOW BAD WAS IT?
TWO DEAD, ONE WOUNDED.
WE GOT OFF LIGHT.

THAT'S NOT OUR PROBLEM.
OUR PROBLEM IS WE'VE BEEN ATTACKED IN OUR HOME, AND THAT CANNOT STAND.

NOT MUCH WE CAN DO ABOUT THAT.
HE'S RIGHT, BOSS. IT'S DOMESTIC.

I DON'T CARE.

WE'RE NOT CHARTERED FOR DOMESTIC WORK, BOSS, YOU KNOW THAT. IT'S THE PURVIEW OF MI5.
FIVE WASN'T ATTACKED, TOM. WE WERE.

THE FOREIGN OFFICE WILL GIVE US BACKING.
AND THE HOME OFFICE WILL OPPOSE.
I CAN SEE WHERE YOU'RE HEADING, BOSS...

... BUT IF S.I.S. GOES MUCKING ABOUT IN A FIVE INVESTIGATION--
THEY CAN INVESTIGATE TO THEIR HEART'S CONTENT, TOM!
THAT'S NOT WHAT I WANT!

WHAT DO YOU WANT, SIR?

RETALIATION.

SIR? THE DEPUTY CHIEF WANTS YOU IN C'S OFFICE.
TELL THEM I'M COMING UP.

I WANT YOU THREE IN THE PIT.
WAIT THERE 'TIL I NEED YOU...

... I'LL CALL WHEN I'M DONE WITH C AND WELDON.

AND WHILE WE WAIT, WHAT? SHARPEN OUR KNIVES?

YOU CAN GET DIGGING, TOM.
AND ANOTHER CRACK LIKE THAT, I'LL FIND MYSELF A NEW HEAD OF SECTION.

DOES THAT MEAN I GET YOUR JOB?
SOD OFF, TARA.

... SHOULD BE HERE IN HALF AN HOUR.
HE'LL MEET WITH CROCKER.

I'M NOT CERTAIN THAT'S *WISE,* SIR...
WHATEVER *HISTORY* EXISTS BETWEEN THEM, THEY'LL BE *PROFESSIONAL.*

PROFESSIONAL ISN'T THE *WORD* I USE TO DESCRIBE...
SORRY TO KEEP YOU *WAITING.*

YOU WERE IN THE OPS ROOM?
YES, SIR.
ANYTHING?

WE'RE STILL WAITING TO HEAR FROM THE *M.O.D.* ABOUT THE WEAPON.
HOPEFULLY THAT WILL GIVE US A *LEAD.*

UNLIKELY, DON'T YOU THINK, PAUL? THESE DAYS ONE CAN BUY A *ROCKET LAUNCHER* AT ANY *CORNER STORE.*
I AM *AWARE,* SIR...
... BUT RIGHT NOW THAT'S ALL WE HAVE.

YOU'LL GIVE WHATEVER YOU LEARN TO FIVE, OF COURSE.
I'LL SHARE IT WITH THEM, YES, SIR.

IT'S AN ACADEMIC DISTINCTION.
I DON'T THINK IT IS.

IT'LL BE THEIR INVESTIGATION.
IT WAS OUR PEOPLE WHO WERE MURDERED.
I'M NOT ABOUT TO LET THOSE PRATS IN FIVE SPEAK FOR THEM.

THOSE PRATS, AS YOU PUT IT, PAUL, ARE OUR COLLEAGUES IN INTELLIGENCE.
IMPLYING THAT DEPARTMENTAL RIVALRY WILL INFLUENCE THE QUALITY OF THEIR INVESTIGATION IS CHILDISH.

DON'T YOU THINK?
IT'S NOT THE QUALITY I'M WORRIED ABOUT, SIR, BUT THE RESULT.

THEY'LL SEE THE RESPONSIBLE PARTIES IDENTIFIED AND IMPRISONED.
I DON'T WANT THEM IMPRISONED...

... I WANT THEM DEAD.

SURE YOU DON'T WANT TO RUN TO THE COMISSARY AND GRAB YOURSELF AN APPLE?
I DO A MEAN WILLIAM TELL.
YOU'RE A RIOT, TOM.
HE'S A RIOT, ISN'T HE?
IF YOU MEAN THE KIND WITH PROPERTY DAMAGE AND LOSS OF LIFE, THEN YES.
I'LL REMEMBER YOU SAID THAT WHEN I'M PREPARING YOUR ANNUAL REVIEW.
YOU DON'T SCARE ME...
... SHE'LL HAVE YOUR JOB BY THE END OF THE DAY.
YOU'LL BE NICE TO ME, WON'T YOU TARA?
DO YOU SWEAR EVERLASTING LOYALTY... TO LIVE AND DIE AT MY COMMAND?
I FEAR I HAVE CONFUSED YOU WITH SOMEONE ELSE.
I THOUGHT YOU WERE TARA CHACE, NOT PAUL CROCKER.

ROCKET HIT THE FIFTH FLOOR?
YES.
WHO WAS WORKING UP THERE?
JILL BARON, ALBERT COOPER, AND A FELLOW FROM MAINTENANCE NAMED RAVI.
BARON AND COOPER WERE ON THE RUSSIAN DESK.
IT'S COINCIDENCE...
... THEY WEREN'T THE TARGET.
NOT SPECIFICALLY, NO...
... WE WERE.
YOU MEAN ALL OF US... THE SERVICE.
VERY DEFT, ED. YOU SHOULD BE A SPY.
IS THE BOSS SERIOUS? ABOUT RETALIATION AND ALL THAT?

... TURN EVERYTHING INTO YOUR OWN PERSONAL CRUSADE?
IT'S NOT MY CRUSADE. IT'S FOR THE GOOD OF THE SERVICE!
IF WE'RE NOT SEEN TO TAKE EVERY MEASURE TO PROTECT AND AVENGE OUR PEOPLE, HOW CAN WE EXPECT THEM TO TRUST US!

THERE IS A LITTLE THING CALLED PATRIOTISM, PAUL. PERHAPS YOU'VE HEARD OF IT?
PATRIOTISM DOESN'T GUARANTEE LOYALTY, IT ONLY INITIATES IT!

AND THE UNSPOKEN COROLLARY TO YOUR CODE OF VENGEANCE IS WHAT, EXACTLY?
BETRAY US AT THE COST OF YOUR LIFE?

IF IT PREVENTS ANOTHER PHILBY OR MACLEAN OR BURGESS, YES, SIR.

I SEE.

AND IF THE WHOLE OF S.I.S. SERVES IN FEAR, THAT'S JUST A HAPPY BY-PRODUCT?

OF COURSE NOT! BUT RELYING ON THE OLD BOY--
THAT'S ENOUGH.

WHY DON'T YOU LEAVE US ALONE, DONALD?

DONALD WELDON IS THE DEPUTY CHIEF.
HE DEMANDS... RIGHTLY... THE RESPECT DUE HIM.

I DO RESPECT HIM.
YOU RESPECT THE POSITION, NOT THE MAN. AN ATTITUDE THAT WILL GET YOU INTO TROUBLE, PAUL.

YOU'RE MARGINALLY EASIER TO REPLACE THAN HE IS.
DON'T FORCE ME TO CHOOSE.
UNDERSTOOD, SIR.

IT SO HAPPENS THAT I AGREE WITH YOU.
AN ATTACK LIKE THIS MUST BE ANSWERED. AND WE MUST BE SEEN TO ANSWER IT.

THEN LET ME USE THE MINDERS TO...
ANSWERING IT DOES NOT MEAN MURDER.

DAVID KINNEY WILL BE IN YOUR OFFICE IN TEN MINUTES.
I EXPECT YOU TO COOPERATE WITH HIM.

I MEAN IT, PAUL.
YES, SIR.

KATE, CALL THE U.S. EMBASSY. FIND OUT IF CHENG IS FREE FOR LUNCH.
CAN I TELL HER WHAT IT'S ABOUT?
SHE'LL KNOW.

DAVID KINNEY IS BEING ESCORTED UP FROM RECEPTION.
ANY CHANCE HE'LL GET LOST ON THE WAY?
THE WARDENS ARE OLD, BUT NOT THAT OLD.

SEND HIM IN WHEN HE GETS HERE.
YES, SIR.

DAVID KINNEY, SIR.
THANKS, KATE.

PAUL.
DAVID.
TAKE A PEW.

BAD BUSINESS. SORRY ABOUT YOUR PEOPLE.
YES. THANKS.
WHAT HAVE YOU GOT?

WE'RE LESS THAN SIX HOURS INTO OUR INVESTIGATION.
WHAT MAKES YOU THINK WE HAVE ANYTHING?

THE FACT THAT YOU'D SOONER EAT BROKEN GLASS THAN ASK FOR MY HELP.

AND THE FACT THAT YOU'D RATHER FELLATE A PONY THAN GIVE IT TO ME.

BUT YES, WE DO HAVE SOMETHING.
AND YOU'RE GOING TO HATE IT.

WELL?

YOUR MINDERS IN THEIR PIT?

DEET DEET

MINDER ONE.

YOU ON YOUR BIKE?
NO...

... D. OPS WANTS YOU IN HIS *OFFICE.*

MINDER TWO TO SEE YOU, SIR.
ROLL HER IN.

SIR?

DON'T THINK YOU'VE MET DAVID KINNEY. HE'S MY OPPOSITE NUMBER AT FIVE.

IT'S A PLEASURE, SIR.
WELL, WE'LL SEE ABOUT THAT.
YOU CAN SIT, TARA.

OUR BROTHERS AT FIVE KNOW WHO GAVE US THE EARLY WAKE-UP THIS MORNING.

GROUP OF RUSSIANS... USED TO WORK FOR A MAN NAMED MARKOVSKY.
RING ANY BELLS?

HE KNOWS ALL ABOUT IT, TARA. DON'T WORRY.

I KILLED HIM.

YES, YOU DID.
QUITE DEFTLY, TOO, FROM WHAT WE'VE HEARD. PROBLEM IS, MARKOVSKY HAD MATES...
... A LOT OF THEM.

FIVE SAYS THE RUSSIANS KNOW WHO PULLED THE TRIGGER.
THEY'RE AFTER US IN GENERAL, AND YOU SPECIFICALLY.

YOU'RE LEAVING OUT THE BEST PART, PAUL.

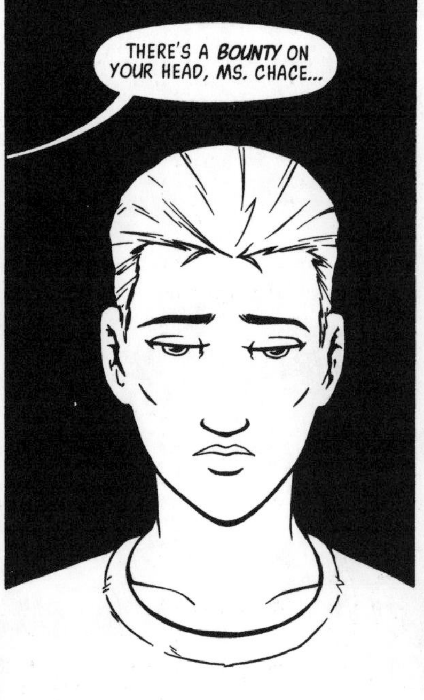
THERE'S A BOUNTY ON YOUR HEAD, MS. CHACE...

... ONE MILLION U.S. FOR THE HEAD OF MINDER TWO.

GET OUT!
WE'RE NOT FINI--
I ALWAYS KNEW YOU WERE A BASTARD, DAVID...
... I JUST DIDN'T KNOW YOU WERE A SADIST, AS WELL.
THEY WANT ME TO BE THE BAIT.
IF THEY MAKE A TRY AT YOU, THEY'LL EXPOSE THEMSELVES.
ONCE THEY'RE IN THE OPEN, WE CAN TAKE THEM...
... MAKE THEM ANSWER FOR THIS MORNING.
ASSUMING I SURVIVE THE TRY.
ASSUMING.

DID YOU KNOW JILL BARON OR ALBERT COOPER?
YES.
COULDN'T STAND EITHER OF THEM.

BUT THE JANITOR... RAVI DIOP...
... HE WAS A NICE MAN.

TELL KINNEY I'LL START WHENEVER HE'S READY.

CHAPTER 3

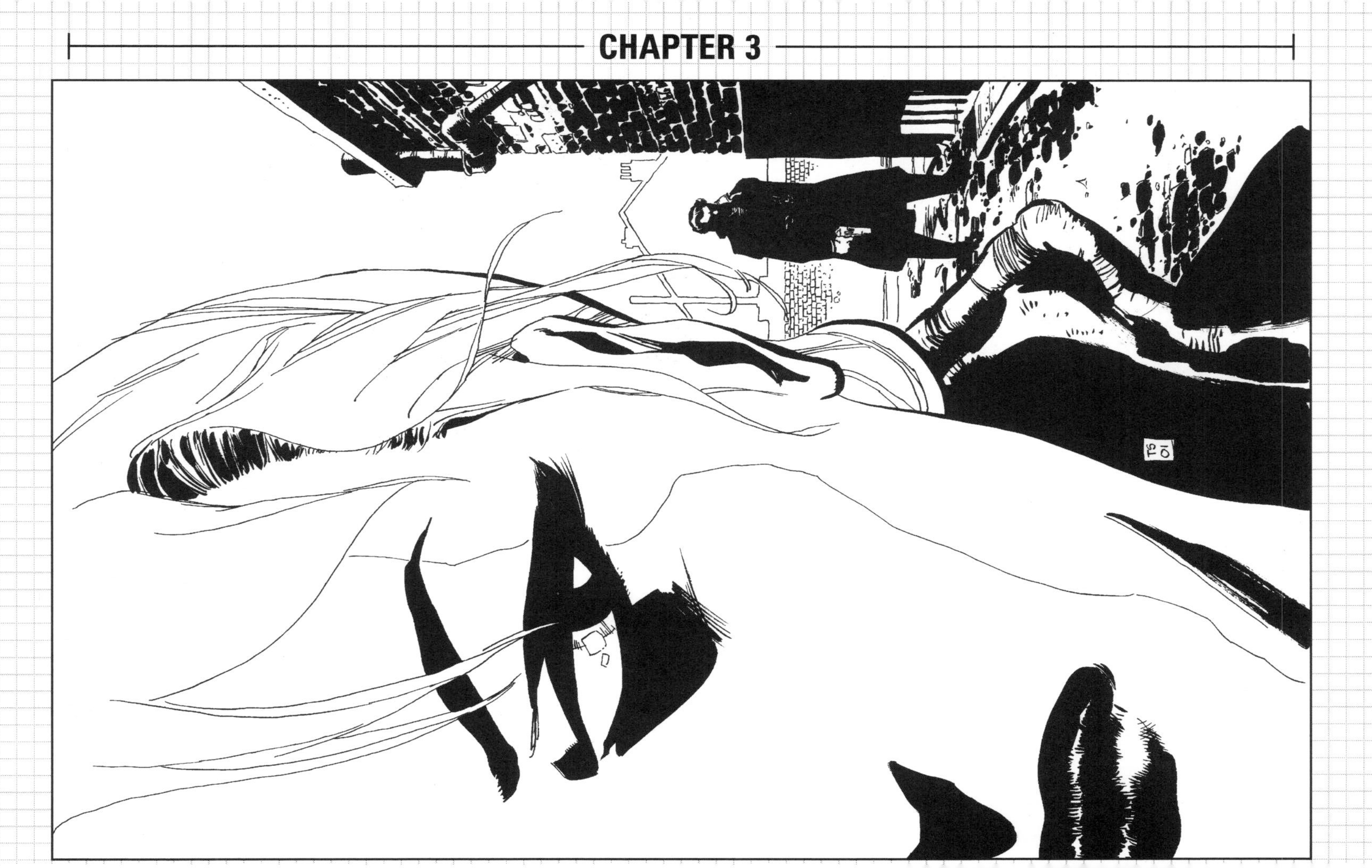

STILL THERE, ROSE?
STILL HERE, TULIP. SEE ANYTHING WORTH REPORTING?
NOT MUCH...
... THOUGH THE BIRD IN THREE-TEN MIGHT BE WORTH WATCHING IF SHE CHANGES FOR BED...
... BUT I HAVE TO REPORT THAT, SADLY, DAISY'S NEIGHBORS ARE ALL DAMN UGLY.
WELL, YOU KNOW WHAT YOU DO, ROSE?
YOU SPY ON DAISY. SURE TO GET AN EYEFUL THAT WAY.
BRILLIANT, TULIP.
THEN DAISY KILLS ME, THE RUSSIANS KILL HER...
... AND YOU'RE SUDDENLY HEAD OF THE SPECIAL SECTION.
AH, YOU'VE SEEN THROUGH MY CUNNING PLAN...

... YOU REALIZE WHAT THAT MEANS, OF COURSE.
I DO, INDEED...

... IT MEANS IT'S TIME FOR A NEW PLAN.
... IT MEANS IT'S TIME FOR A NEW PLAN.

TULIP, ROSE, IT'S DAISY.
SHUT THE BLOODY HELL UP.

THANK YOU.
DAISY OUT.

I feel JUSTIFIED in a certain TARTNESS of TONE.

I am, after all, worth one MILLION dollars.

Or at least, that's what the RED MAFIYA is willing to PAY for my head.

Not REALLY the same thing, is it?

One wonders how they go about making THAT particular request.
Wanted: SIS Officer Tara Chace's HEAD, preferably on a PLATTER...

... BODY optional...

... SAT ON HER ALL NIGHT AND THERE WAS NO SIGN OF ANYTHING...

... ED'S WATCHING HER PLACE NOW.
YOU GET ANY SLEEP?
AS YOU KNOW, I AM A MASTER OF THE ART OF WANG-O-WANG, WHICH ALLOWS ONE TO SLEEP WITH HIS EYES OPEN.
I EVEN DREAMED. SOME OF THEM WERE DIRTY. WANT TO HEAR ONE, BOSS?

YOU'RE ABOUT HALF THE WIT YOU THINK YOU ARE, TOM.
WHAT ABOUT MINDER TWO?
LIGHTS WENT OFF AT TWENTY-THREE HUNDRED, ABOUT...

--THANKS, KATE--
-- WHAT TARA DID AFTER THAT, I'VE NO CLUE.
NOT MUCH BLOODY USE, ARE YOU?
KATE!

PAUL?
DID YOU CALL CHENG?
OF COURSE I DID.
AND?
AND SHE'LL BE FREE AFTER ONE THIS AFTERNOON.
NOT BEFORE?

NO. NOT BEFORE.

I SHOULD FIRE HER.

DO THAT AND YOU'LL DESTROY US ALL.
DESPITE WHAT KATE WOULD HAVE YOU BELIEVE, TOM, SHE DOES NOT RUN THE SERVICE.
YOU'RE JUST CRANKY BECAUSE RUSSIANS ARE TRYING TO KILL YOUR GIRL.

I SHOULD HAVE SENT YOU TO KOSOVO, TOM.
YEAH, PROBABLY. BUT I WOULD'VE MISSED THE SHOT ON MARKOVSKY, AND THEN WHERE WOULD WE BE?

GO GET SOME SLEEP, THEN RELIEVE ED.
YOU COMMAND, AND I OBEY.
CLASSIFIED

PAUL!
YOU'RE GOING TO BE LATE.

CALL THE EMBASSY, TELL HER I'LL BE IN THE PARK.
SHE'S PROBABLY ALREADY LEFT--
SHE HASN'T LEFT, SHE'S RUNNING LATE, TOO.

AND WHEN MINDER THREE GETS IN, TELL HIM I'LL SEE HIM WHEN I GET BACK--
PAUL.

SIR.
HEADING OUT?
MEETING WITH CHENG.

A MINUTE IN YOUR OFFICE, PLEASE.

KATE?
I'LL LET HER KNOW.

I SAW A MEMO FROM MATERIEL THIS MORNING ABOUT THREE WALTHER P88s.
DID YOU ARM THE MINDERS?
CHACE IS BEING HUNTED BY THUGS IN THE MIDDLE OF LONDON, SIR...
... OF COURSE I ARMED THE MINDERS.
WE CAN'T HAVE S.I.S. RUNNING ABOUT LONDON LIKE EXTRAS FROM SOME AMERICAN ACTION FILM, PAUL.
YOU GET AWAY WITH THAT BEHAVIOR ON STATION, NOT AT HOME. NOT HERE...
AND CERTAINLY NOT WHEN KINNEY AND THE REST OF FIVE ARE BREATHING DOWN OUR NECKS.
YOU HAVE TO DISARM THEM.
AND WHEN THE RUSSIANS MAKE THEIR TRY, WHAT IS CHACE SUPPOSED TO DO?
BAT HER EYES AND ASK THEM SWEETLY TO NOT MURDER HER TOO MUCH?
I'M NOT SAYING IT'LL BE EASY, PAUL.
BUT WALLACE, CHACE, AND KITTERING COMPRISE YOUR SPECIAL SECTION...
... PERHAPS IT'S TIME THEY PROVE HOW SPECIAL THEY ARE.

DAISY? IT'S TULIP...

... YOUR PHONE IS ABOUT TO RING.
BRRT
BRRT

BRRT
THAT WAS VERY CLEVER, TULIP.
CAN YOU TELL ME WHAT HAPPENS NEXT WEEK ON CASUALTY?
SORRY?

CHACE.
TARA? IT'S PAUL.
YES, SIR?

I JUST HAD A MEETING WITH THE DEPUTY CHIEF.
HE'S ORDERED THE MINDERS TO TURN IN THEIR WEAPONS.

ED WILL COLLECT YOUR GUN WHEN TOM REPLACES HIM.
VERY GOOD, SIR.

I'M MEETING WITH CHENG.
WE'LL COME UP WITH SOMETHING, DON'T WORRY.
YES, SIR.

DAISY? IT'S ROSE.
TULIP'S ON HIS WAY TO THE DOOR...

YOU'RE THE ONLY MAN I LET KEEP ME WAITING.
YOU LET YOUR AMBASSADOR KEEP YOU WAITING.
ACTUALLY, I DON'T.
WHAT HAPPENED?
WELDON WANTED A PIECE OF ME.
DOESN'T LIKE THE MINDERS GOING ARMED IN LONDON.
CAN'T SAY I BLAME HIM. THEY START SHOOTING, EVERYONE ON YOUR FLOOR WILL NEED TO UPDATE A RESUME.
OH, I KNOW HE'S CORRECT, ANGELA.
I JUST WISH HE WASN'T SO DAMN SMUG ABOUT IT.
LIKE YOU KNEW ABOUT AMES.
NO FAIR! YOU DIDN'T KNOW ABOUT PHILBY, MACLEAN, BURGESS...
POINT TAKEN.
CAN YOU HELP?
HELP HOW?
GIVE ME SOME BACK-UP.
DON'T YOU HAVE FIVE BACKING YOU? WHAT'S HIS NAME? KINNEY?
DAVID KINNEY, YES, AND THAT'S NOT THE HELP I'M LOOKING FOR.
KINNEY WANTS AN ARREST.

IS THAT WHAT YOU WANTED TO MEET ABOUT?
NO, BUT IT MAKES THIS MORE PRESSING.
YOU KNOW THE SITUATION?
RED MAFIYA WANTS CHACE'S HEAD BECAUSE OF WHAT SHE DID TO MARKOVSKY.
SHOULD I EVEN ASK HOW YOU KNOW?
HEY, I'M CIA. WE KNOW EVERYTHING.
I WANT THEM DEAD.
JESUS CHRIST, PAUL!
THEY ATTACKED US IN OUR HOME, ANGELA.

CAN YOU HELP?
WHAT DO I LOOK LIKE, LADY MACBETH?

ONE OF *MY* PEOPLE IS BEING *HUNTED* BECAUSE OF A *FAVOR* I DID FOR THE *CIA.*
CHACE TOOK MARKOVSKY AT LANGLEY'S REQUEST.

FOR WHICH LANGLEY IS *GRATEFUL,* PAUL.
BUT THEY'RE NOT GRATEFUL ENOUGH TO ALLOW *ME* TO AUTHORIZE A *COVERT* ACTION IN DOWNTOWN LONDON.
YOU COULD *ASK.*

I *KNOW* WHAT THEY'LL SAY. THEY'LL SAY *NO.*
AND WITH GOOD REASON. CAN YOU IMAGINE THE POLITICAL *SHITSTORM* WE'D BE IN IF ANYTHING *LEAKED?*

FORGET THE *DAILY MIRROR,* IT'D BE IN THE WASHINGTON FUCKING POST.
NO WAY THE NEW PRESIDENT WILL LET THAT COME *CLOSE* TO HAPPENING. HIS POSITION IS TOO *SHAKY* RIGHT NOW.

ALL RIGHT, IF YOU CAN'T GIVE ME PERSONNEL, CAN YOU GIVE EQUIPMENT?
IF YOU'RE GOING TO SAY WHAT I THINK YOU'RE GOING TO SAY...

THREE PISTOLS, DOESN'T MATTER THE MAKE, AS LONG AS THEY WORK.
YOU'VE GOT TO HAVE UNTRACEABLE WEAPONS.
HELL NO! CIA GUN OR CIA GUNMAN, IT'S THE SAME PROBLEM, PAUL!

YES, WE DO. THEY'RE FOR USE BY OUR PEOPLE.
SO YOU'VE GOT NOTHING FOR ME?
ONLY MORE VERBAL DARTS.

SADLY, CHACE ISN'T IN A POSITION TO PLAY GAMES.
WELL, IT MIGHT GET HER OUT OF HER FLAT. AND THE KIDS ALWAYS HAVE THE BEST TOYS.

I'VE GOT TO GET BACK TO THE EMBASSY.
YES.

GOOD LUCK WITH IT.

PUB

MICS
SMOKE DOG
WERS
Sidekicks
NEW

MICS
SMOKE DOG
WERS

TOYS & COMICS
SALE

KATE!

PAUL?

WHERE'S MINDER THREE?

HE'S IN THE *PIT,* HAS BEEN FOR OVER AN *HOUR* NOW. PAUL--

GOOD, MAKE SURE HE DOESN'T *LEAVE.*

ACTUALLY, DON'T, I'LL CALL HIM.

PAUL, DAVID KINNEY--

RUN THAT DOWN TO *DESIGN...*

... TELL THEM I WANT IT BY *TONIGHT,* AND TO MAKE THEM LOOK DAMN *PROPER.*

HOPE YOU WERE WAITING LONG.
NOT VERY.
WHAT'S THE HOLD-UP?

HOLD-UP?
CHACE HASN'T MOVED IN TWO DAYS. WHAT ARE YOU WAITING FOR?

I WANT MY PEOPLE IN PLACE BEFORE SHE GOES UNDER FIRE, IF THAT'S ALL RIGHT.
MY PEOPLE ARE ALREADY IN PLACE, PAUL.

THEN YOU UNDERSTAND MY FEARS.

I UNDERSTAND YOU'RE CODDLING HER. SHE STAYS INDOORS, THE RUSSIANS WON'T MOVE ON HER.
SHE'S SUPPOSED TO BE DRAWING THEM OUT.

AND IN TIME SHE WILL.
TIME WE DON'T HAVE.

I WANT THIS DONE TONIGHT.
ORDER HER INTO MOTION AND QUIT STALLING!

DO I NEED TO SPEAK TO *WELDON?*
YOUR *NOSE* DOES SEEM *REMARKABLY* FREE OF *SHITE.*

RIGHT.

YOU'RE STILL *MATES,* I SEE.
SHUT UP.
HE'S GOING TO *WELDON.*

WHY?
HE'S ACCUSING ME OF *CODDLING* CHACE...

... WANTS THE *DC* TO ORDER ME TO ORDER HER TO GIVE THE *RUSSIANS* THEIR *SHOT.*
WHAT ABOUT THE *OTHER* THING?
READY BY *FIVE.*

GOOD.
ED? IT'S D. OPS. MY *OFFICE,* PLEASE...

...HOW MANY?
TULIP THERE?
AT LEAST TWO, SO DOUBLE THAT NUMBER.

JUST ARRIVED.
I'LL BE RIGHT IN, THEN.

HE'S COMING.
GOOD.
YOU WANT A DRINK?

DOESN'T STRIKE ME AS THE TIME.
ME EITHER.

SORRY ABOUT THAT.
WE'RE SURE IT'S THEM?
THEM OR FIVE.

IT'S THEM.

SO WHAT IS THE GOOD WORD FROM MASTER CROCKER?
HE OFFERS US TOYS AND INSTRUCTIONS.
WE'RE EACH TO TAKE ONE OF THESE...

... AND THEN WATCH TARA GO FOR A WALK BY THE WATER.

ARE THESE PELLET GUNS?
YES. WE'RE TO BLUFF WITH THEM.
BLUFF.
YES.
GETS WORSE. KINNEY GOT THE DC TO ORDER TARA INTO THE OPEN...
... ASSURED HIM THAT FIVE WOULD PROVIDE ADEQUATE BACK-UP.

FIVE WANTS ARRESTS. THEY'LL TRY TO TAKE THE RUSSIANS ALIVE.
WHICH MEANS THEY'LL WAIT UNTIL AFTER THE TRY.

I'LL GET MY COAT.

YOU'VE GOT TWO, DAISY.

UNDERSTOOD.

TULIP, GO.

IN MOTION.

ROSE, DAISY. TWO DOWN...

... I'LL CALL HOME AND HAVE THEM COLLECTED...

... THE REST ARE YOURS.
Two of them.

Wallace and I can TAKE two of them.

Just pick the MOMENT.

Just don't PANIC.

That's all it's about.
The FEAR.

It's not about THEM. It's NEVER about them.

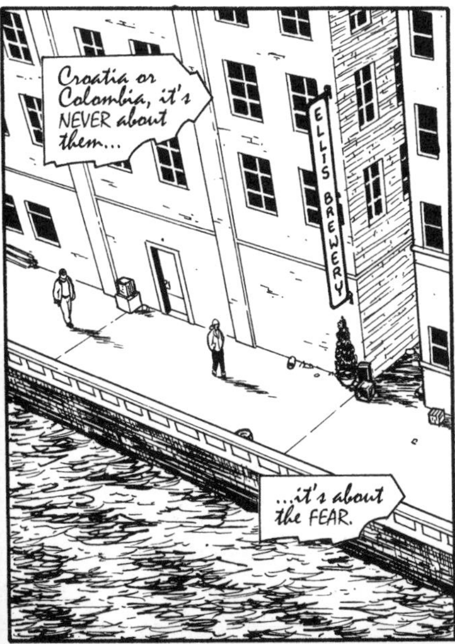
Croatia or Colombia, it's NEVER about them...
ELLIS BREWERY
...it's about the FEAR.

Wait.
Wait.

Wait...
...closer...
...closer...
...oh damn
oh dammit
too FAR...
DROP IT!
DROP IT--
...not going to going to
shoot close the distance
run close the distance
run RUN—
BLAM!
BLAM!
BLAM!

CHAPTER 4

There's a trick, they teach it to you at the School.
When someone pulls a GUN on you, they say...
... CHARGE at him like a bloody LUNATIC...
... It's the LAST thing they EXPECT and most of them can't hit WATER from a SUBMARINE anyway...
...and repeat to yourself OVER and OVER that you're doing this for QUEEN and COUNTRY.

TARA.
IT'S DONE.

THERE WAS ONE MORE.
YEAH, HE'S NOT GOING TO BE TROUBLE.
ONE OF THE ROUNDS THAT MISSED YOU FOUND HIM.
CHRIST.
IT'S HOLLYWOOD WHAT DOES IT, YOU ASK ME.
THESE BLOKES SEE A MOVIE WHERE EVERYONE'S PRANCING ABOUT, FIRING CANNONS WITH ONE HAND...
... THEY'RE MORE CONCERNED WITH LOOKING GOOD DURING A GUNFIGHT THAN WITH LIVING THROUGH THE DAMN THING.
WHAT THEY DON'T REALIZE, YOU SEE, IS THAT EVERY BULLET HAS TO GO SOME-WHERE.
HEY-- TOM?
YES, LOVE?
... NOTHING.
NEVER MIND.
AH, GOOD MASTER KINNEY AND ETCETERA HAVE ARRIVED.

WHAT THE HELL HAPPENED HERE?

YOU! CHACE!
I WANT AN ANSWER, BY GOD!

YOU STUPID BITCH!
YOUR ORDERS WERE TO DRAW THEM OUT, NOT TO ENGAGE!

I KNEW CROCKER WOULD TRY SOMETHING LIKE THIS...

... TURNING HIS THUGS LOOSE TO PURSUE A VENDETTA...
MISTER KINNEY!

SOD FUCKING OFF.

YOU HAVE A PROBLEM WITH MY PERFORMANCE, YOU'RE FREE TO TAKE IT UP WITH MY D. OPS...

... AT WHICH POINT I'LL BE DELIGHTED TO TELL THE HOME OFFICE ABOUT HOW YOU ARRIVED JUST AFTER THE NICK OF TIME.

DAMN BITCH.

... TO THE *FARM* FOR INTERROGATION.

THEY'RE UNDER GUARD NOW, AND KINNEY HAS HIS *QUESTIONERS* EN ROUTE.

AND THE MINDERS?

I SENT THEM HOME AFTER THEY FILED THEIR REPORTS.

WALLACE AND CHACE WILL BE BACK IN THE *PIT* ON *STAND-BY* BEFORE *NOON*.

NOT *KITTERING*?

EDWARD'S WITH DOCTOR CALLARD, THEN *OFF* FOR THE REST OF THE *DAY*.

THE REPORT SAID NOTHING ABOUT KITTERING TAKING AN INJURY.

THAT'S CORRECT, SIR.
HE DID, HOWEVER, KILL ONE OF THE RUSSIANS WITH HIS BARE HANDS.

AH, RIGHT.
WELL, HE DIDN'T HAVE ANY CHOICE, DID HE, PAUL?
NO, SIR.

WAS THERE SOMETHING ELSE, PAUL?
WHAT WILL HAPPEN TO THE RUSSIANS AFTER FIVE FINISHES THEIR INTERROGATION?

DON'T KNOW, TO BE HONEST, AND DON'T MUCH CARE.
EXTRADITION BACK TO MOSCOW MOST LIKELY.
WHY?

I'M LOOKING FOR YOUR APPROVAL ON THIS.
IS THIS IMMEDIATE?

CLOSE OF PLAY WILL BE FINE, SIR.
VERY WELL.
THAT'LL BE ALL FOR NOW.

PAUL!
SIR?

CONGRATULATE THE MINDERS FOR ME.
JOB WELL DONE.
YES, SIR.

TOM?
Hmm?
YOU EVER SEEN CALLARD?
THE MADWOMAN OF THE SECOND FLOOR?
NOT FOR A WHILE, NO.

COMING UP ON *FOUR* YEARS, IN FACT.

YOU DIDN'T SEE HER AFTER *KOSOVO?*

WASN'T *TIME.*
SICK *LEAVE* FROM THE *INJURY.* THEN THIS *THING* WITH THE *RUSSIANS.*

YOU SHOULD MAKE AN *APPOINTMENT.*

I'M FINE, TOM.

... MAKE THIS AND THEN I'M OFF.
WHO SAID YOU COULD GO?
IT'S TWENTY PAST SIX ON A FRIDAY, PAUL...
WHERE IS HE?!

DEPUTY CHIEF TO SEE YOU, SIR.
HULLO, SIR.

WILL YOU NEVER LEARN?
CAN I ASSUME THE PROPOSAL WILL GO TO 'C' WITHOUT YOUR ENDORSEMENT?

IT WON'T GO TO 'C' AT ALL, PAUL!
YOU WILL NOT MOUNT, I WILL NOT ENDORSE, AND 'C' WILL NOT AUTHORIZE AN ASSASSINATION OF THIS KIND.

WHAT SORT OF ASSASSINATION WILL YOU ENDORSE, THEN, SIR?
PERHAPS WE CAN WORK SOMETHING OUT.

THE RUSSIANS ARE IN CUSTODY.
IT'S OVER. IT'S FINISHED.

SO YOU HAD BEST FORGET ABOUT YOUR VENDETTA...

... AND TURN YOUR ATTENTION TO OPERATIONS ELSEWHERE.
GOOD EVENING.

HE GONE?
YES.
THEN CALL CHENG. TELL HER I NEED TO TALK TO HER TONIGHT.

SHE'S DINING WITH A TRADE GROUP AT EIGHT...

Nozemack's
N
N

KATE MADE IT SOUND LIKE THE WORLD WAS ENDING.
IS THE WORLD ENDING?
I NEED A FAVOR.
CHIP?

I WAS IN THE MIDDLE OF A VEAL ESCALOPE AND YOU OFFER ME A PIECE OF FRIED POTATO.
WISH I COULD DO BETTER. ON MY WAGE, I CAN HARDLY AFFORD TO SAY "VEAL ESCALOPE."

MY CUP OF PITY IS OVERFLOWING.
WHAT DO YOU NEED THAT CAN'T WAIT UNTIL TOMORROW?
I THINK FIVE IS GOING TO LOSE THE RUSSIANS.

DAMMIT IT'S *COLD.*
LOSE THEM *HOW?*
NOT SURE. BUT WELDON WAS TALKING ABOUT *EXTRADITION* TO *MOSCOW.*
CAT FOOD

I SPOKE WITH RAYBURN, AND HE'S HEARD RUMORS THAT THERE'S A *DEAL* ALREADY IN *PLACE.*
DOESN'T KNOW WITH *WHOM.*
D. INT HEARS A *RUMOR* AND THEREFORE YOU *RUIN* MY DINNER.
LET IT *GO,* PAUL, LET IT BE SOMEONE ELSE'S *PROBLEM* FOR *ONCE.*

IT'S NOT WHAT I *WANT.*
I TRIED TO GET *OFFICIAL* SANCTION, BUT *WELDON* STOPPED ME BEFORE I EVEN HAD *MY BOOTS* ON.

THEY'RE AT THE *FARM* NOW, BUT IT WON'T BE FOR *MUCH* LONGER. NO IDEA WHERE THEY'LL BE MOVED NEXT. NO IDEA WHEN.
PAUL, WHY ARE YOU TELLING ME THIS? WHAT DO YOU *WANT?*

FINE.
BUT REMEMBER, *YOU* ASKED *ME.*

... TO ADDRESS DONALD'S CONCERNS.

THIS IS AN ALARMING PROPOSAL, PAUL.
IT SHOULD BE, SIR.
THE PURPOSE OF THAT OPERATION IS TO PUT THE FEAR OF GOD INTO ANY GROUP THAT WOULD HUNT AND KILL OUR AGENTS.

IT GOES TOO FAR.

I DISAGREE, SIR. IT DOESN'T GO FAR ENOUGH.
I BEG YOUR PARDON?
WE WERE ATTACKED IN OUR HOME.
THEY PUT A BOUNTY ON THE HEAD OF MINDER TWO.

WE ARE HMG'S SECRET INTELLIGENCE SERVICE, YET THESE HOODS ATTEMPTED TO TERRORIZE US.
WE MUST STRIKE BACK, SIR.

WE OWE IT TO CHACE, AND TO ALL OF OUR AGENTS.
NOT JUST FOR WHAT WE'VE ASKED OF THEM, BUT FOR WHAT WE MAY ASK OF THEM.

UNLESS OUR AGENTS KNOW WE WILL FIGHT FOR THEM, HOW CAN WE ASK THEM TO GIVE THEIR LIVES FOR US?
WE MUST STRIKE BACK.

EVEN KNOWING THIS GOVERNMENT'S POLICY ON ASSASSINATION, YOU PROPOSED THIS OPERATION ANYWAY.

I DON'T KNOW IF THAT SPEAKS OF YOU WELL, OR AS A FOOL.
WE HAVE TO PUNISH--
THEY ARE BEING PUNISHED, PAUL.

THE FARM ISN'T REALLY HARD TIME, THOUGH, IS IT?
THE FARM IS NOT THE END OF THEIR JOURNEY.

THEN THEY ARE GOING BACK TO RUSSIA?

DON'T EVEN CONSIDER IT, PAUL.
THERE ARE OTHER THINGS AT STAKE HERE BESIDES YOUR OVER-DEVELOPED SENSE OF DOMINION.

AND I'VE TOLD YOU ALREADY, YOU'RE REPLACEABLE.

P.A. TO D. OPS.
KATE, IT'S D. OPS. HOW MANY MINDERS ARE IN THE PIT?
YOU'VE GOT THE COMPLETE SET.
GET THEM INTO THE OPS ROOM QUIETLY. I'LL BRIEF THEM WHEN I GET BACK.
BY QUIETLY YOU MEAN "WITHOUT WELDON FINDING OUT"?
JUST DO IT, KATE.
OF COURSE, SIR.

ED, IF YOU CAN STOP MOLESTING LEX FOR A FEW MINUTES, I'D APPRECIATE YOUR ATTENTION.
IT WAS NOTHING, BOSS. TOTALLY INNOCENT.
IF LEX IS INNOCENT, I'M YOUR MOTHER.
THEY'RE MOVING THE RUSSIANS OFF THE FARM TONIGHT.
IF IT'S GOING TO BE DONE, IT'S GOT TO BE DONE THEN.
IF ANY OF YOU HAS TROUBLE WITH THIS, SAY IT NOW.
NO, SIR.
YOU DIDN'T GET CLEARANCE, DID YOU?
NO, I DIDN'T. YOU'RE FREE TO GO IF YOU'D RATHER, TOM.
I'M NOT GOING ANY-WHERE.
GLAD TO HEAR IT.
IT NEEDS TO LOOK LIKE AN ACCIDENT...

WE'VE BEEN HAD.

THEY DIDN'T SHOW?

NO ONE SHOWED.
WALLACE RADIOED FROM OUTSIDE THE FARM, SAYS THE WHOLE PLACE IS SHUT TIGHT.

LET ME GET DRESSED.
ED, HEAD BACK TO THE OFFICE. TARA, YOU STAY.
DO I GET TO COME INSIDE, THEN?

MY WIFE WOULDN'T APPROVE.

YOU HAVE OPTICS?
BRING THEM.
BINOCULARS IN THE BOOT.
BASTARDS.

PAUL.
THEY'D ALREADY ARRANGED THE DEAL WITH FIVE--
YOU'RE BLOODY CIA IN LONDON, ANGELA!
YOU SHOULD HAVE TOLD LANGLEY TO FUCK OFF.
I'M TRYING TO TELL YOU IT WASN'T THE COMPANY THAT DID THIS!
KINNEY WENT TO THE FBI BEFORE THE RUSSIANS WERE EVEN IN CUSTODY.
I DIDN'T FIND OUT UNTIL I WENT TO DO YOU A FAVOR YESTERDAY.
YOU SHOULD HAVE WARNED ME OFF.
... A BREAK... NOT GOING TO SCREW THE FBI...
... SCREW US INSTEAD...
... BASTARD TRIED TO GET MY AGENT KILLED...
WORD OF ADVICE FOR YOU, MISTER KINNEY...

... NEXT TIME YOU FIND SOMEONE SHOOTING AT YOU...
... AND YOU'RE UNARMED...
... TRY RUNNING TOWARDS THE SHOOTER...
... AND PRAY THE SHOOTER ISN'T ME.

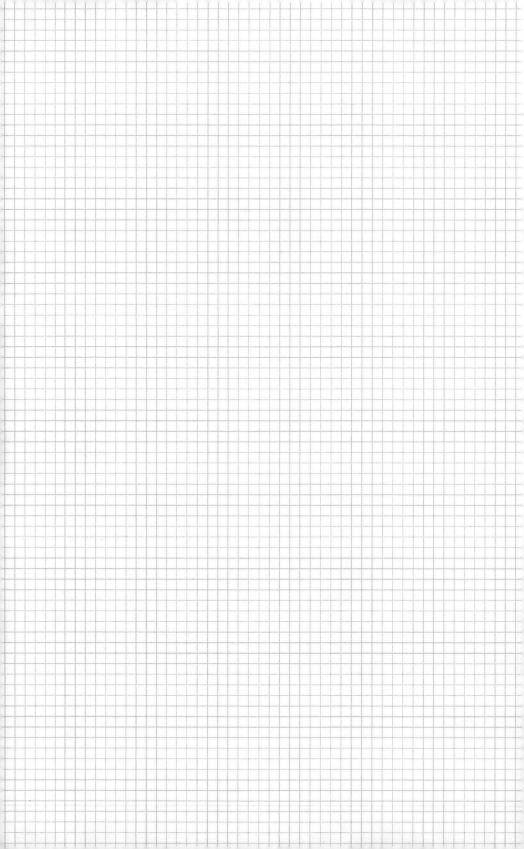

OPERATION: MORNINGSTAR

WRITTEN BY
GREG RUCKA

PENCILLED BY
BRIAN HURTT

CHAPTER 1 INKED BY
BRYAN LEE O'MALLEY

CHAPTERS 2 & 3 INKED
BY CHRISTINE NORRIE

LETTERED BY
SEAN KONOT

ORIGINALLY EDITIED BY
JAMIE S. RICH

ROSTER

C—Ubiquitous code-name for the current head of S.I.S.. Real name is Sir Wilson Stanton Davies.

DONALD WELDON—Deputy Chief of Service, has oversight of all aspects of Intelligence gathering and operations. Immediate superior to Crocker.

PAUL CROCKER—Director of Operations, encompassing all field work in all theaters of operations. In addition to commanding individual stations, has direct command of the Special Section–sometimes referred to as Minders –used for special operations.

TOM WALLACE—Head of the Special Section, a Special Operations Officer with the designation Minder One Responsible for the training and continued well-being of his unit, both at home and in the field. Six year veteran of the Minders.

TARA CHACE—Special Operations Officer, designated Minder Two. Entering her third year as Minder.

EDWARD KITTERING—Special Operations Officer, designated Minder Three. Has been with the Special Section for less than a year.

OPS ROOM STAFF

OTHERS

ALEXIS—Mission Control Officer (also called Main Communications Officer)– responsible for maintaining communications between the Operations Room and the agents in the field.

RON—Duty Operations Officer, responsible for monitoring the status and importance of all incoming intelligence, both from foreign stations and other sources.

KATE—Personal Assistant to Paul Crocker, termed P.A. to D.Ops. Possibly the hardest and most important job in the Service.

ANGELA CHANG—CIA Station Chief in London. Has an unofficial intelligence-sharing arrangement with Crocker.

SIMON RAYBURN—Director of Intelligence for S.I.S. (D. Int), essentially Crocker's opposite number. Responsible for the evaluation, interpretation, and dissemination of all acquired intelligence.

DAVID KINNY—Crocker's opposite number at M.I.5, also called the Security Services, with jurisdiction primarily confined to within the U.K.

CHAPTER 1

KABUL, AFGHANISTAN.

-- HANDS OFF ME--
-- SOMEONE TO A *PHONE*--
-- KNOW I'M A *JOURNALIST*--
QUIET, YES? QUIET?
WE WILL CALL *NAMES* AND IF YOURS IS A NAME THAT IS *CALLED* YOU WILL STEP *FORWARD.*

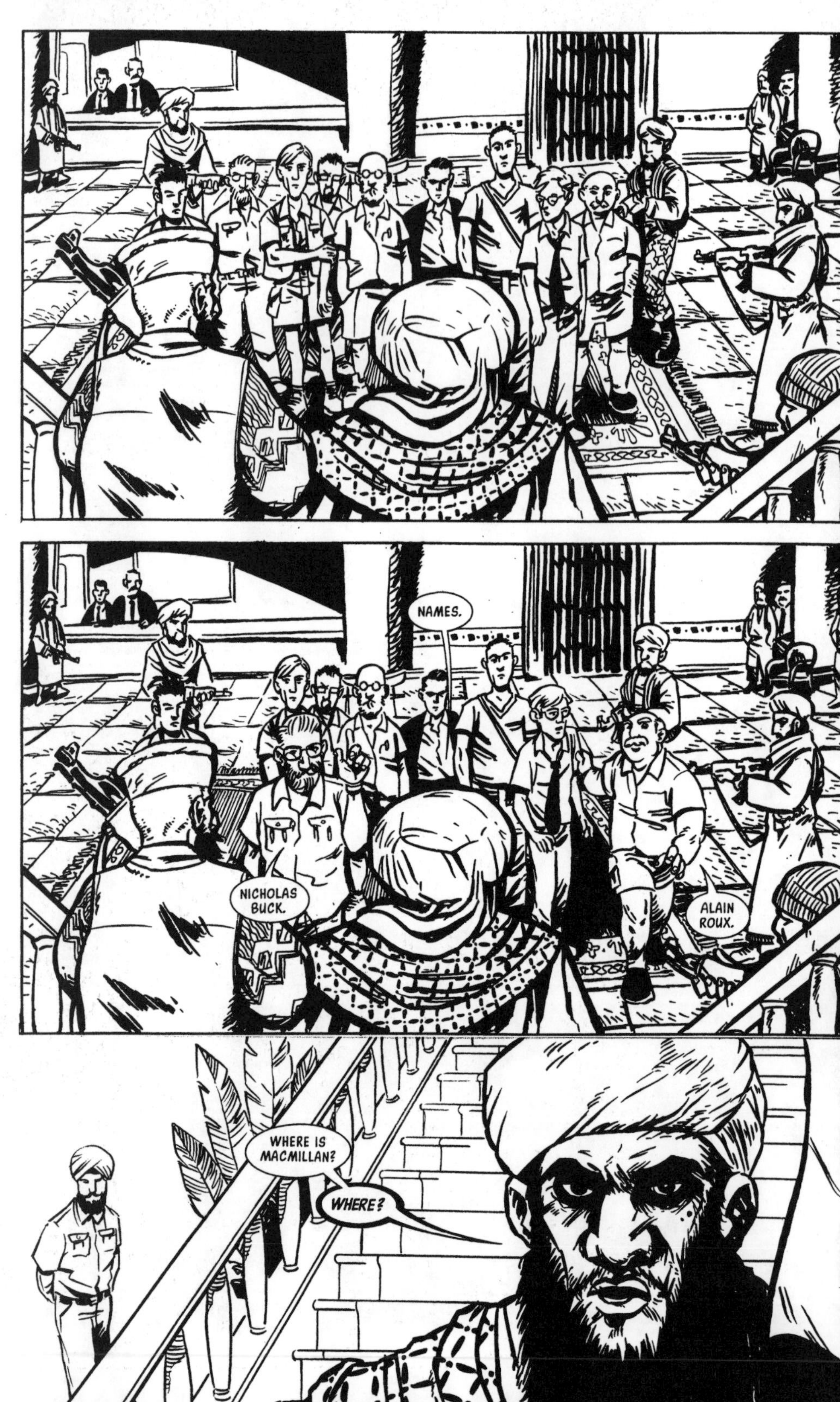
NAMES.
NICHOLAS BUCK.
ALAIN ROUX.
WHERE IS MACMILLAN?
WHERE?

THEN THAT IS HOW IT WILL *BE.*
YOU ARE *ALL* UNDER ARREST--
HEY! GET *OFF*--
-- INTERNATIONAL *NEWS*--
I'M *HERE.*

DAVID MACMILLAN OF THE REUTERS NEWS AGENCY?
LAST I CHECKED. PROBLEM?

NOW *WAIT* JUST-- *nuuh*--

YOU ARE ACCUSED AS A *SPY* AND A *COMMUNIST...*
... AND WILL BE *TRIED* AND *EXECUTED* AS SUCH.

LONDON.
WHY DON'T YOU HAVE A SEAT?
MAKE YOURSELF COMFORTABLE
Cambridge University
Eleanor Grace Callard
YOU CAN SMOKE IF YOU LIKE.
TOP SECRET- PERSONNEL
CHACE, Tara
I'LL BE TAKING NOTES, IF YOU DON'T MIND.
First Session
YOU DON'T MIND, DO YOU?
First Session
-Reticent
WHY DON'T YOU SIT DOWN?
PLEASE.

WHAT ARE YOU WRITING?
JUST MY NOTES.
THEY'RE *CONFIDENTIAL*, JUST BETWEEN YOU AND *ME*.
THEN I CAN READ THEM?
CERTAINLY.
HAVE I GOT IT *RIGHT* SO FAR?
-Reticent
-Suspicious

SO FAR.
THEN WE HAVE THE FOUNDATION OF TRUST, WOULDN'T YOU SAY?
I WOULDN'T GET CARRIED AWAY, DOCTOR.
WHY ARE YOU HERE, TARA?
YOU KNOW WHY, DOCTOR.
MY HEAD OF SECTION ORDERED ME TO SEE YOU.
WALLACE, RIGHT?
YES.
AND PRESUMABLY, HE DID SO WITH D. OPS' BLESSING?
YES.

Hmm.
ACCORDING TO YOUR FILE, YOU'RE NOT DUE FOR A REVIEW FOR ANOTHER FOUR MONTHS.
THAT'S RIGHT.
HAVE YOU DEVELOPED A FEAR OF FIRE, TARA?
WHAT?
DON'T BE ABSURD.
I ASK BECAUSE YOU'VE WORRIED THAT FAG TO PIECES.
WHY DON'T WE START BY TALKING ABOUT OPERATION BROKEN GROUND?

KATE?
YES, MASTER?
WHO HAS THE MUGABE PACT?

GOOD MORNING, SIR.
YES, SIR...
KATE, IS PAUL IN?
C'MON IN, SIMON.

DIRECTOR INTELLIGENCE TO SEE YOU, SIR.
YES, I'D NOTICED, THANK YOU, KATE.

YOU'LL HAVE TO FORGIVE HER. SHE NEEDS TO FEEL USEFUL.
SOMEONE AROUND HERE SHOULD.

WHAT CAN I DO FOR YOU?
HAS THE OPS ROOM PASSED YOU ANYTHING FROM KABUL?

NOT SINCE DELHI STATION STARTED TREELINE.
THE UNITED FRONT CONTACT LIST?
YES...

... PICK UP FROM ONE OF OUR STRINGERS BY THE DELHI NUMBER TWO. THEN OUT THROUGH DELHI STATION TO US.
WHY?

THE STRINGER, IT'S DAVID MACMILLAN?
YES.

ONE OF MY PEOPLE JUST PULLED THIS FROM THE INTERNET.

HOW OLD?
SIX HOURS AT THE MOST.
THE OTHER TWO, BUCK AND ROUX? WHO WERE THEY WORKING FOR?
THE TALEBAN WILL HAVE THEM EXECUTED BEFORE DAWN.
BEST AS WE CAN TELL, NO ONE.
THOUGHT YOU'D WANT TO SEE IT.
ROTTEN FOR THEM.
YES.
HELL.
I APPRECIATE IT, THOUGH WHEN I FIND OUT WHY THIS DIDN'T COME THROUGH THE OPS ROOM I'LL HAVE SOMEONE'S HEAD.
PROBABLY BECAUSE THEY HAVEN'T HEARD YET.
WAITING ON THE DELHI NUMBER TWO'S REPORT, MOST LIKE.
BUSINESS IN THE MODERN WORLD, PAUL. CNN HAS BETTER INTELLIGENCE THAN WE DO.

GOOD LUCK WITH IT.
THANKS, SIMON.

PAUL?
IT'S D. OPS. INFORM 'C' I'M COMING UP.
OF COURSE IT'S BLOODY URGENT.

WHAT DO YOU NEED?
INFORM THE DEPUTY CHIEF'S OFFICE THAT I'M GOING UP TO 'C'...

... THEN GET THE MINDERS TO THE OPS ROOM, CRASH BRIEF ON AFGHANISTAN...

... I'LL JOIN THEM AS SOON AS I'M ABLE.

TOM? MINDERS TO THE OPS ROOM.
YOU'RE ON YOUR BIKES.

THINK THAT'S MY PROBLEM, THEN?
WHICH BOOK?
SEXUAL DYSFUNCTION AND STRESS.
GET A LOT OF THAT AROUND HERE?
MORE DYSFUNCTION THAN SEX.
A LOT OF YOUR COLLEAGUES HAVE PERFORMANCE ISSUES RELATED TO THE JOB.
IT'S DIFFICULT TO FEEL AROUSAL WHEN YOU'VE SPENT THE DAY CATALOGUING RAPE CAMPS IN EASTERN EUROPE.
THAT'S ANALYSIS, NOT OPS.
I SAID THAT'S ANALYSIS. THAT'S INT. RAYBURN'S PEOPLE.
NOT OPS.

ARE YOU SEEING ANYONE NOW?
YOU'RE NOT MY TYPE, I'M AFRAID.
SO YOU'RE SINGLE, THEN.
IT'S IN THE FILE. IT'S ALL IN THE BLOODY FILE.
YES, BUT I'M ASKING YOU.
AND I'M SAYING IT'S IN THE BLOODY FILE.
WAS GENERAL MARKOVSKY THE FIRST MAN YOU'VE KILLED?

HE WAS THE FIRST MAN I EVER KILLED LIKE THAT.
THE FIRST I'VE EVER BEEN ORDERED TO ASSASSINATE.
NO.
YES.
YOU DIDN'T LIKE IT.
JESUS.
ARE THERE REALLY PEOPLE WHO DO?
YES.
CLEARLY YOU'RE NOT ONE OF THEM, SO YOU'RE AHEAD OF THE GAME.
I CAN'T-- I CAN'T SLEEP...
... NOT WELL, AT LEAST.

ALCOHOL?
IN BUCKETS.
YES, WELL, VOLUME IS EVERYTHING.
WIDE MOUTH ON THOSE BUCKETS?
SO, TELL ME, DOC...
... WILL I EVER PLAY THE PIANO AGAIN?
YOU'RE PLAYING IT NOW.
TRUST ME, I'VE HEARD FAR WORSE IN THIS ROOM.
BDEET--
BDEET--
PARDON ME.
CALLARD.
YES, SHE'S HERE.
YES, I'LL TELL HER.
YOU'RE WANTED IN THE OPS ROOM, I'M AFRAID.

... PICKED THE STORY UP ON CNN...
... OVERLAND COVER WITH DOCUMENTATION...
KABUL
... STATEMENT BY MULLAH MUHAMMAD OMAR TO THE EFFECT THAT--
TOM?
WHAT'S HAPPENED?
TREELINE WENT BUST.
JESUS.
FANCY A TRIP TO KABUL, THEN?
MORE THAN YOU CAN IMAGINE, ED.
I'VE BEEN PRAYING FOR A CRACK AT THOSE BASTARDS.

IT'S A SPECIAL OP.
VERY GOOD, SIR.
OPERATION DESIGNATED MORNINGSTAR.
KABUL
OPERATION: MORNINGSTA_
RON, I NEED THE SOONEST FLIGHT TO DELHI.
ALREADY DONE, SIR...
... BRITISH AIRWAYS FLIGHT 143, DEPARTS HEATHROW OH-SIX-FIFTY-FIVE TOMORROW, ARRIVES DELHI TWENTY-TWO TEN LOCAL.
YES, SIR.
TWO SEATS.
MINDERS ONE AND THREE TO BRIEF.
FULL COVER, WITH DOCUMENTS.
NO ARMS.
VERY GOOD, SIR.
ED? TOM?...
... YOU'LL BE TRAVELING AS IRRIGATION TECHNOLOGY SALESMEN, WITH THE DELHI NUMBER TWO AS YOUR TRANSLATOR.
THAT'S CORRECT...
THAT'S DENNIS AVASTI?

... AND WHEN IS THE DEPUTY CHIEF GETTING BACK?
HE SHOULD BE IN HIS OFFICE NOW.

TELL HIM I NEED TO SEE HIM RIGHT AWAY.

IN MY OFFICE.
OLIVER? IT'S KATE...

SHUT THE DOOR.
D. OPS NEEDS TO SEE THE DEPUTY CHIEF RIGHT AWAY...

I'M FIT TO RUN.
IF I DIDN'T THINK THAT, I'D HAVE FIRED YOU ALREADY.

THEN WHY ARE YOU SENDING THE BABY INSTEAD OF ME?
YOU KNOW I CAN BACK TOM BETTER THAN ED CAN, I'VE GOT MORE FIELD EXPERIENCE THAN--
ED CAN HOLD HIS OWN.

DAMMIT, PAUL!
IT'S THE TALEBAN FOR GOD'S SAKE!
AND THAT'S PRECISELY WHY I CAN'T SEND YOU!

HOW THE HELL DO I PLACE YOU, TARA? DO I COVER YOU HEAD TO TOE IN A BURQA?
DO WE SAY TOM'S YOUR BROTHER AND PRETEND YOU'RE BEING ESCORTED BY A RELATIVE?

EVEN IF MEN AND WOMEN WEREN'T FORBIDDEN TO MIX PUBLICLY...
ANY IDEAS?

WE COULD FIND A WAY. SEND ME IN WITH U.N. COVER--
WOULDN'T WORK, AND YOU KNOW IT.
AND WE DON'T HAVE TIME, TARA.

MACMILLAN WAS SUPPOSED TO GIVE AVASTI THE LIST OF UNITED FRONT CONTACTS IN THE SOUTH.
FOR THE OFFENSIVE IN THE WINTER, I'VE READ THE BRIEF.

WE DON'T KNOW WHERE THE LIST IS.
MACMILLAN MAY HAVE HAD IT ON HIM WHEN HE WAS ARRESTED.

BUT AVASTI--
HE COULDN'T CLEAR ANY OF THE DEAD DROPS. THE MILITIA WAS ON ALERT ALL THROUGHOUT THE CITY.

IF MACMILLAN HAD THE LIST ON HIM, THAT MEANS THE TALEBAN'S GOT IT.
IF HE MANAGED TO CACHE IT, IT'S IN THE OPEN, SO THEN THEY'RE SEARCHING FOR IT.

WE LOSE THAT LIST, THE WHOLE NETWORK FOLDS.
THE TALEBAN GETS IT, EIGHTY-SIX MEN AND WOMEN WILL BE EXECUTED FOR TREASON.

WE DON'T HAVE TIME TO PLACE YOU.
IT'S TOM AND ED, AND THAT'S FINAL.
SIR? THE DEPUTY CHIEF CAN SEE YOU NOW.

TELL HIM I'M ON MY WAY UP, KATE.
YES, SIR.

THERE'S ALWAYS *ANOTHER* SPECIAL OP, TARA.
SURE.

-- RESULT OF CONTINUED ECONOMIC SANCTIONS IN THE REGION.
IN AFGHANISTAN THIS MORNING, JOURNALISTS NICHOLAS BUCK, DAVID MACMILLAN, AND ALAIN ROUX WERE EXECUTED BY THE TALEBAN GOVERNMENT AFTER BEING FOUND GUILTY OF ESPIONAGE.
MACMILLAN, A BRITISH NATIONAL AND TWENTY-TWO YEAR VETERAN CORRESPONDENT, HAD BEEN CHARGED SPECIFICALLY WITH SPYING FOR S.I.S..
THE FOREIGN OFFICE HAS DENIED THE ALLEGATION.
IN RELATED NEWS, A REPORT RELEASED BY AMNESTY INTERNATIONAL TODAY ESTIMATES...
... THAT TENS OF THOUSANDS OF AFGHANI WOMEN SUFFERING FROM VARIOUS MEDICAL CONDITIONS FACE CERTAIN DEATH IF CONTINUED TO BE DENIED MEDICAL TREATMENT BY THE TALEBAN GOVERNMENT...

CHAPTER 2

DELHI, INDIA.
TOM! TOM!
OVER HERE!
THERE YOU GO, DENNIS, BLOWING MY COVER IN THE MIDDLE OF THE AIRPORT.
AND THERE YOU GO, TOM, OVER-REACTING AS ALWAYS.
DESPITE THE MEMORY OF YOUR COLONIAL BOOTHEEL...
... INDIA IS NOT ENEMY GROUND.
HE SAYS THAT, BUT DON'T LET HIM FEED YOU A VINDALOO.
ED KITTERING, MEET DENNIS AVASTI. ONE OF THE FEW MEN WHO CAN STAND A MINDER IN HIS PRESENCE.
DELIGHTED TO HEAR THAT.
A PLEASURE.
WE MUST HURRY IF WE'RE GOING TO CATCH THE FLIGHT TO PESHAWAR.
AS IT IS, WE WON'T BE ABLE TO CROSS THE BORDER UNTIL TOMORROW.
EVEN GIVEN THE URGENCY OF THE SITUATION--
DIDN'T YOU HEAR, DENNIS...?
... THE BASTARDS EXECUTED MACMILLAN THIS MORNING...

TARA?
0458 GMT
0928 ZONE
TEN-LETTER WORD FOR 'FIRST *SEXUAL REVOLUTION*,' BEGINNING WITH AN '*L*'?
KABUL
OPERATIÓN: MORNINGSTAR
STATUS: FREE RUN
"LYSISTRATA."
AH, THAT'S THE TRICK.
MORNING, FRED.

RON.
YOU'RE IN EARLY.
MORNINGSTAR.
OF COURSE.
DELHI STATION CONFIRMS ARRIVAL IN PESHAWAR EARLY THIS MORNING.
THEY SHOULD BE DUE FOR THE BORDER CROSS ANY TIME NOW.
KHYBER ROUTE?
THAT WAS THE PLAN.
I'LL LEAVE YOU TO IT, THEN, SHALL I?
THAT'LL BE FINE.
FRED?
HOW LONG SHE BEEN HERE?
SINCE THREE...
... I DON'T THINK OUR MINDER TWO IS A HAPPY GIRL.

KHYBER PASS
‹... TOLD THEY HAD THE NECESSARY PERMISSIONS AND EVERYTHING WAS IN ORDER.›
ISLAMIC EMIRATE OF AFGHANISTAN
‹HAVE THEM EXIT THE VEHICLE.›
HE ASKS THAT YOU GET OUT OF THE CAR.
DID YOU EXPLAIN THAT WE'RE ON BUSINESS?
I DID, SIR, BUT HE STILL REQUIRES YOU TO EXIT THE VEHICLE.
WELL, I HARDLY SEE THE POINT...
... BUT WE'RE ALREADY RUNNING LATE.
I WILL SEE IF I CAN EXPEDITE THINGS.
‹THESE PICTURES DO NOT LOOK THE SAME AS THE MEN.›
‹I ASSURE YOU, THEY ARE THE SAME.›
‹NO, THEY DO NOT LOOK THE SAME.›
United Kingdom of
HOLLAND
THOMAS
BRITISH
13 MAR
19 MAY
T<GBRHOLLAND<<T
United Kingdom o
RYAN
E<GBREDW
‹I CANNOT GRANT ENTRY IF THEY DO NOT LOOK THE SAME.›
‹PERHAPS THEY HAVE BETTER PICTURES?›
‹OF COURSE, I UNDERSTAND.›
‹I WILL ASK.›

IC EMIRATE
GHANISTAN

HE ASKS IF YOU HAVE *BETTER* DOCUMENTATION.
PERHAPS IN YOUR *WALLETS?*
I... SEE...
YES. WELL.

‹THEY HAVE *LICENSES,* YOU SEE?›

... BLOODY TALKING ABOUT ME LIKE I CAN'T HEAR THEM!
I'M A SPY FOR GOD'S SAKE!
BUT IT WAS A VALID QUESTION, DON'T YOU THINK?
YOU NORMALLY DON'T REPORT TO WORK UNTIL NINE, ISN'T THAT TRUE?
THERE'S AN OPERATION RUNNING IN AFGHANISTAN, DOCTOR CALLARD. RUNNING RIGHT NOW.
WHAT ELSE AM I SUPPOSED TO DO?
AT THREE IN THE MORNING? I'D THINK YOU SHOULD BE SLEEPING.
YES, WELL, WE'VE DISCUSSED THAT ALREADY, HAVEN'T WE?
I COULDN'T SLEEP.
SO YOU WENT TO THE OPS ROOM.
YES.
THIS OPERATION IN AFGHANISTAN...
MORNINGSTAR.
IF YOU SAY.
YOU WANTED TO GO?
DESPERATELY.

D. OPS FELT THAT I WOULD BE USELESS IN THE FIELD.
BUT YOU'RE HERE.
AFGHANISTAN.
NOT THE EASIEST PLACE IN THE WORLD TO BE A WOMAN.
YOU AGREED WITH D. OPS' DECISION?
I DIDN'T LIKE IT, BUT YES.
THE BEST THING FOR THE MISSION WAS SENDING TOM AND ED.
BUT...?
BUT...
BUT IT WAS A CHANCE TO DO SOMETHING GOOD...
... MY CHANCE TO DO SOMETHING GOOD.

WHAT MAKES MORNINGSTAR DIFFERENT, TARA?
THE TALEBAN. YOU'VE PROBABLY HEARD OF THEM.
HOW THEY'RE STONING WOMEN FOR SHOWING THAT MOST EROTIC OF BONES, THE ANKLE?
HOW THEY'RE PRODUCING WHOPPING PILES OF HEROIN TO BE SOLD HERE IN THE U.K.?
HOW THEY'RE HARBORING AND FUNDING OSAMA BIN LADDEN?
LITTLE THINGS LIKE THAT.
I'D CERTAINLY WANT THEM TO PAY.
TOO RIGHT.
MORE THAN I'D WANT TO KILL AN EX-RUSSIAN GENERAL AS A FAVOR TO THE CIA, CERTAINLY.
SO YOU UNDERSTAND.

BUT MARKOVSKY WAS RUSSIAN MOB.
HE WAS SELLING GUNS TO TERRORISTS... HE WAS SELLING DRUGS.
THIS MORNING, WHEN YOU WENT TO THE OPS ROOM. WHAT WERE YOU THINKING?
ASKED AND ANSWERED, DOCTOR.
NOT REALLY, NO.
YOU WENT HOME. YOU COULDN'T SLEEP. YOU HAD A FEW DRINKS. YOU STILL COULDN'T SLEEP.
YOU MUST HAVE BEEN KNACKERED, BUT YOU WENT TO THE OPS ROOM.
WHY?
I SIMPLY...
... I DIDN'T KNOW WHERE ELSE TO GO.
ARE YOU LONELY, TARA?
NOT... LONELY...
... JUST ISOLATED.

KATE SAYS YOU WANTED TO SEE ME, SIR?
WHAT'S THE STATUS ON MORNINGSTAR?
MINDERS ONE AND THREE AND THE DELHI NUMBER TWO SHOULD BE JUST NOW REACHING KABUL.
NO CONFIRMATION?
IT'S A FREE RUN. I'M EXPECTING A CALL FROM WALLACE THIS EVENING.
IT'LL BE OPEN CODE, BUT I'LL HAVE MORE DATA THEN.
ONCE IN KABUL, WHAT THEN?
THEY'LL START CLEARING THE DEAD DROPS, HOPING TO LOCATE THE LIST OF UNITED FRONT CONTACTS.
PRESUMING THAT THE MILITIA HASN'T ALREADY GOTTEN THEIR HANDS ON IT?
I DON'T THINK THEY HAVE, SIR.
D. INT HASN'T REPORTED ANY ARRESTS OR MASS EXECUTIONS, WHICH WOULD BE WHAT WE'D EXPECT IF THE NETWORK HAD BEEN BLOWN.
UNLESS THEY'RE SITTING ON THE LIST, WAITING TO SEE WHO COMES TO COLLECT IT.
THAT'S ALWAYS A POSSIBILITY, SIR.
WE'LL KNOW SOON ENOUGH. AS I SAID, TOM AND ED ARE ALREADY IN KABUL.

THE TALEBAN HAS USED EVERY TRICK TO GOAD THE INTERNATIONAL COMMUNITY INTO RECOGNIZING THEIR AUTHORITY.

THE AMERICANS JUST SENT THEM IN EXCESS OF THIRTY MILLION DOLLARS TO FIGHT THEIR SO-CALLED "WAR ON DRUGS."

THE AMERICANS...

IT AMOUNTED TO A TACIT ENDORSEMENT OF THE REGIME.

IF THE MINDERS ARE ARRESTED, WE COULD FIND OURSELVES BLACKMAILED INTO A DIALOGUE THAT WILL DO THE SAME THING.

WE CANNOT ALLOW THAT, PAUL.

AND THE EIGHTY-SIX MEN AND WOMEN ON THAT LIST, WE JUST ABANDON THEM?

AREN'T YOU THE MAN WHO WAS PREACHING LOYALTY ABOVE ALL ELSE JUST A FEW MONTHS AGO?

YOU WERE ADVOCATING MURDER THEN, YOU MAY RECALL.

MORNINGSTAR HAS C'S BLESSING.

I WON'T ABORT WITHOUT A DIRECTIVE FROM HIM.

IT'S YOUR OPERATION, NOT HIS. YOURS IS THE CAREER THAT WILL SUFFER THE RESULT.

I'M ONLY TRYING TO HELP YOU, PAUL.

I'M SURE THE UNITED FRONT APPRECIATES IT AS MUCH AS I DO.

KABUL.
THINK I SHOULD PICK ONE OF THOSE UP, THEN?
I WOULDN'T...
... THEY MIGHT TAKE YOU FOR AN AMERICAN.
HOW WE DOING IN THE REAR, ED?
WE'RE STILL COMFORTABLE...
... I THINK THEY'RE THE COURTESY CREW, RATHER THAN AN OFFICIAL PARTY.
BECAUSE THE OFFICIAL PARTY IS SEARCHING OUR ROOMS AS WE SPEAK.
A SAFE ASSUMPTION.

WE SHOULD WATCH THE ENGLISH FROM HERE.
MATCH ABOUT TO START, YOU THINK?
YOU WANT TO GIVE IT A MISS, COME BACK LATER?
THERE IS A TIME CONCERN.
HELL.
SOMETHING'S GOT THEM EXCITED.
COULD BE OUR OPPORTUNITY TO GET IN.
GO BACK TO THE HOTEL, ED.
IF WE'RE NOT BACK FOR THE CALL, TELL THE BOSS IT'S A BUST AND THEN GET THE HELL OUT OF TOWN.

HERE YOU GO.
THANK YOU. I'D LIKE ANOTHER.
MIGHT WANT TO FINISH THAT ONE FIRST, DEAR.
RIGHT.
THAT'LL D
WON'T BE A SECOND.

ANOTHER, PLEASE.
RIGHT WITH YOU, SIR.
BAD DAY AT THE *OFFICE*, THEN?
LET ME *FINISH* THIS AND WE'LL *GO*.
UHM.
RIGHT.
... I'M *RICHARD*, BY THE WAY.
TARA.

TOM, COME ON.
THEY JUST...
... JESUS, WHY?
THEY DON'T NEED A REASON, TOM.

IF I WERE A *BETTER MAN*, I'D HAVE ASKED THIS *FIRST.*
BUT DO YOU WANT TO *TALK* ABOUT IT?
NO.

TOM? HOW'S BUSINESS?
ENLIGHTENING, BUT FRUITLESS...
... SO FAR, WE HAVEN'T FOUND ANY INTERESTED BUYERS.
YOU'VE SPOKEN TO ALL OF OUR PROSPECTS?
0104 GMT
0534 ZONE
KABUL
OPERATION: MOR
STATUS: FREE R
ONLY GOT TO THREE OF THEM TODAY. IT WAS BUSY.
THERE ARE A FEW MORE WE'LL LOOK INTO TOMORROW.
AND THE COMPETITION? HAVE THEY HAD ANY SALES?
THEY'VE BEEN SNIFFING AROUND, BUT I THINK IT'S NORMAL CURIOSITY. NOBODY'S TRIED THE HARD SELL YET.
YES, WELL, THE SUPERVISOR HERE THINKS THEY MAY BE TRYING TO UNDERCUT US, YOU UNDERSTAND?
IT WAS ALWAYS A POSSIBILITY. BUT I'VE SEEN NO SIGNS OF IT.
THEN KEEP AT IT, AND HOPEFULLY TOMORROW WILL BRING MORE LUCK.
TALK TO YOU SOON.
THAT WAS TOM?
YOU SHOULD BE AT HOME, TARA.

BUT THEY'RE BEING WATCHED?
THEY CLEARED TWO OF THE DROPS, DIDN'T FIND ANYTHING.
THEY'LL TRY FOR THE OTHER TWO TOMORROW.
TOM THINKS IT'S STANDARD SECURITY, NOT A TARGETED OPERATION.
IF ANOTHER SPECIAL OP COMES UP I'LL HAVE TO SEND YOU, AND I'D RATHER PUT YOU IN THE FIELD WITH SOME SLEEP.
GO HOME, TARA.
YES, SIR.
GOOD NIGHT.
GOOD NIGHT, SIR.

DIDN'T EXPECT YOU UNTIL AFTER NOON.
I GOT *BOOTED* FROM THE OPS ROOM.
BEEN HERE *ALL* NIGHT, HAVE YOU?
DID SOMETH HAPPEN WIT MORNINGSTA

I LET A PERFECT STRANGER TAKE ME TO HIS HOME LAST NIGHT.
DID YOU ENJOY IT?
NOT PARTICULARLY.
DID YOU THINK YOU WOULD?
NOT PARTICULARLY.
SO YOU WERE PUNISHING YOURSELF.
OR WAS IT SOMETHING ELSE?
I DON'T... KNOW WHAT TO DO.
I DON'T KNOW WHAT I SHOULD DO.
DO YOU BELIEVE IN YOUR JOB, TARA?
SOMETIMES.
MOST TIMES.
BUT YOUR FAITH WAS TESTED IN KOSOVO.
YOU WANTED MORNINGSTAR BECAUSE YOU HOPED IT WOULD BRING IT BACK.
NOW YOU'RE LEFT WITH DOING IT YOURSELF.
I DON'T KNOW IF I CAN.
I CAN'T SOLVE YOUR PROBLEM, TARA, I CAN ONLY POINT YOU IN THE RIGHT DIRECTION.
THEN SHOW ME, DAMMIT.
WHAT DO I DO?
YOUR JOB, OF COURSE.

... AND WHERE ARE WE OFF TO TODAY, THEN?
THERE ARE SOME PROSPECTS JUST OUT OF TOWN I THOUGHT YOU GENTLEMEN WOULD WANT TO EXAMINE.

CHAPTER 3

PAGMAN, 19 KM N.W. OF KABUL.
... ASININE CHOICE FOR A DLB, IF YOU ASK ME.
I DIDN'T.
IT'S NOT THERE.
SO FAR NO... JUST ANOTHER FEW SECONDS...
IT'S NOT BLOODY THERE.
THIS IS THE LAST DROP, TOM. IT HAS TO BE HERE.
NO, IT DOESN'T.
IF MACMILLAN MANAGED TO DITCH THE LIST, HE SURE AS HELL DIDN'T DO IT 23 KLICKS OUTSIDE OF KABUL.
IT'S IN THE CITY IF IT'S ANYWHERE.
BUT WE CLEARED ALL THE DROPS IN THE CITY.
YOU THINK I DON'T KNOW THAT?
IT'S NOT IN A DLB, ED...
... IT'S OUT IN THE SODDING OPEN...

LONDON.
MINDER TWO AS REQUESTED, SIR.
SHOW HER IN, KATE.

AND IF WE COULD GET SOME COFFEE, I WON'T HAVE TO FIRE YOU.
I OBEY.
PARK IT, TARA.

YOU HEARD THE LATEST ON MORNINGSTAR?
JUST THE MCO TRANSCRIPT WHEN I CAME IN THIS MORNING.
THEN YOU KNOW TOM AND ED HAVE CLEARED ALL THE DROPS, AND THEY HAVEN'T FOUND THE LIST.
YES, SIR.

THE PLAN FOR TREELINE HAD BEEN FOR MAC ILLAN TO BUMP-PASS TO AVASTI AT THE HOTEL, PHYSICAL CONTACT--
-- THANK YOU, KATE--
-- THERE WAS NEVER A PLAN TO DLB THE LIST.

IF THE TALEBAN HAD IT, THEY'D HAVE GONE AFTER THE CONTACTS ALREADY, WOULDN'T THEY?
D. INT SAYS THE NETWORK IS STILL INTACT.
THEN EITHER THEY DON'T HAVE THE LIST, OR THEY DO AND HAVEN'T USED IT YET.

THE LATTER IS THE DEPUTY CHIEF'S THEORY.
HE'S OF THE OPINION THAT TOM AND ED ARE BOUND FIRST FOR INTER-NATIONAL NEWS AND THEN FOR A FIRING SQUAD.

WE'RE CERTAIN MACMILLAN ACTUALLY *HAD* THE LIST IN HIS POSSESSION?
YES, THAT'S BEEN CONFIRMED.
THEN HE MUST HAVE KNOWN THE MILITIA WAS WAITING AT THE HOTEL, AND DITCHED IT NEARBY.

THEY CAN'T REALLY GO WANDERING THROUGH THE STREETS OF KABUL HOPING TO FIND IT THOUGH, CAN THEY?
CERTAINLY NOT IF THEY'RE ALREADY BEING WATCHED.
WHICH THEY ARE.

I WANT YOU TO DIG UP WHATEVER YOU CAN ON MACMILLAN.
MAYBE THERE'S SOMETHING WE'RE MISSING ABOUT HIM THAT'LL GIVE US A POINTER.
YES, SIR.

TOM AND ED HAVE BEEN ON THE *GROUND* FOR *TWO* DAYS, TARA.
IF THE TALEBAN *IS* SETTING US UP, THEY'RE NOT LIABLE TO WAIT MUCH LONGER.
YOU THINK THEY'LL BE PICKED UP EVEN *WITHOUT* THE LIST?
I THINK THESE ARE PEOPLE WHO COULD CARE *LESS* ABOUT *EVIDENCE*.

I'M GIVING IT UNTIL DAYLIGHT TOMORROW, THEN THEY'RE ABORTING, LIST OR NO.
WITH THE LIST WOULD BE *PREFERABLE*.
UNDERSTOOD, SIR.

SEND A RUNNER DOWN TO THE PIT WITH MACMILLAN'S FILE, SO TARA CAN START REVIEWING IT.
BY YOUR COMMAND.

KATE.
HMM?
CALL CALLARD, FIND OUT WHEN I CAN COME AND SEE HER.

DON'T TELL ME YOU'RE OFF YOUR NUT *TOO?*
SHUT UP.

P.A. TO D. OPS. D. OPS IS WONDERING IF THE DOCTOR MIGHT HAVE TIME FOR HIM LATER TODAY?
VERY GOOD, THANK YOU.

WELL?
SHE CAN SEE YOU *NOW.*

SHOULDN'T BE TOO LONG.
DON'T RUSH ON *MY* ACCOUNT.

... HAVE HEAT ON DOWN HERE?
IT IS ON.
SAYS YOU.
TA.

... EXPLAIN IT AGAIN, TOM.
RULES OF TRADECRAFT.
WHAT'S THE FIRST THING YOU DO AFTER YOU LOAD A DROP?
PLACE YOUR DLB LOADED SIGN. HANDKERCHIEF OFF THE FLOWER POT, THAT KIND OF THING.
BUT MACMILLAN NEVER SIGNALED DROP LOADED.
MACMILLAN WASN'T THE MOST RELIABLE AGENT I'D EVER WORKED WITH, TOM. HE MIGHT'VE FORGOTTEN.
CARRYING THE UNITED FRONT CONTACT LIST?
HE'D HAVE BEEN SO SCARED HE'D NEVER EVEN HAVE CONSIDERED NOT PLAYING BY THE BOOK.
HE WAS SUPPOSED TO PASS THE LIST TO YOU, PHYSICALLY.
SO IT WAS ON HIM RIGHT UP UNTIL HE SPOTTED THE MILITIA AT THE HOTEL.
I WAS IN THE LOBBY WHEN HE WAS TAKEN. HE DIDN'T DROP IT THERE.
OUTSIDE, SOMEPLACE.
RIGHT. AND SOMEPLACE NEAR.

I COULD START SWEEPING.
I'M MARGINALLY LESS CONSPICUOUS THAN YOU TWO.
BAD IDEA, DENNIS.

HE'S RIGHT. WE'RE ALL BEING WATCHED.
ANY ONE OF US GOES WANDERING, WE'LL CATCH MORE ATTENTION.
AND EVEN IF YOU DID FIND THE LIST, THE CITIZEN'S MILITIA WOULD BE ON YOU BEFORE YOU KNEW IT.

SO NOW WHAT?
OUR GIRL IN LONDON IS WORKING ON IT NOW. IF SHE FINDS SOMETHING, WE'LL NEED A PLAN TO GET PAST OUR WATCHERS.

THIS GIRL.
WHAT CAN SHE POSSIBLY DO FROM THREE THOUSAND MILES AWAY?

START THINKING ON IT, MY LADS.

I'VE GOT ABLUTIONS TO PERFORM.

KATE? MINDER TWO FOR D. OPS...
... WHEN'S HE DUE BACK?
NO, IT'S NOT URGENT.
JUST LET HIM KNOW I WENT OUT...
... I'VE GOT A COUPLE OF THINGS I WANT TO CHASE DOWN.
NO, I'LL CALL IN IF I FIND ANYTHING.
NO, MACMILLAN HAD A BIRD IN THE CITY...
INDIGO, SO LOW-RISK, BUT IT'S WORTH A LOOK...
... RIGHT. THANKS, KATE.

MS. ALLEN?
MS. ALLEN, ARE YOU THERE?
SHE'S OFF.
DO YOU KNOW WHEN SHE'LL BE BACK?
NONE OF MY BUSINESS, REALLY.
THINK HER *BOYFRIEND* DUMPED HER.
DO YOU KNOW WHERE I CAN FIND HER?
SHE WORKS DOWN THE MARKS AND SPARKS. THAT'S IF SHE'S STOPPED *CRYING.*
BEEN NOTHING BUT *TEARS* FROM HER FOR THE LAST TWO DAYS.
PERHAPS I'LL TRY HER THERE, THEN.

... DOESN'T REALLY TELL ME HOW SHE'S FARING, DOES IT, ELEANOR?
WHAT DO YOU WANT ME TO SAY, PAUL? YOU SENT HER TO KOSOVO TO SHOOT A MAN IN COLD BLOOD.
YOU WOULDN'T WANT HER IN THE SECTION IF THAT DIDN'T BOTHER HER.
I WANT YOU TO TELL ME IF I'M GOING TO GET HER BACK OR NOT.
I'M NOT CERTAIN I KNOW WHAT THAT MEANS. YOU HAVE HER NOW.
YOU'D HAVE FIRED HER ALREADY IF YOU THOUGHT THAT.
IF SHE'S GOT MISSION TWITCH--
PAUL...
... WOULD YOU EVEN BE ASKING THESE QUESTIONS IF WE WERE TALKING ABOUT WALLACE?
HER GENDER ISN'T AT ISSUE, ELEANOR. HER JOB IS.
STILL, YOU SENT HER TO KOSOVO. NOT WALLACE. NOT KITTERING.
YOU KNEW WHAT SHE WOULD DO THERE.
WALLACE CAN'T HIT WATER FROM A BOAT, AND KITTERING'S TOO NEW TO THE SECTION.
I SENT CHACE BECAUSE I KNEW SHE COULD GET THE JOB DONE.
THEN YOU'VE ANSWERED YOUR OWN QUESTION.

SHE'S LOOKING FOR A REASON TO FEEL GOOD ABOUT HERSELF, PAUL, AND SHE CAN'T FIND THAT IN THE JOB BECAUSE IT'S JUST NOT THERE.
FOR ANY OF US, ACTUALLY.
IT HAS TO COME FROM HER ABILITY. SHE HAS TO SEE HERSELF AS A GOOD OFFICER AGAIN.
SO WHAT DO I DO? GIVE HER FLOWERS AND A PAT ON THE BACK?
LORD, NO. SHE'D SEE IT FOR EXACTLY WHAT IT WAS, WHICH IS FALSE.
TREAT HER JUST AS BEFORE. THE WHOLE SECTION LIVES AND BREATHES FOR YOUR RESPECT AND YOUR APPROVAL, AS IT IS.
SHE HAS BOTH OF THOSE THINGS.
YES, BUT SHE HAS TO BELIEVE SHE'S EARNED THEM.
IT WON'T TAKE MUCH, JUST A SMALL VICTORY.
SOMETHING THAT CAN'T BE GUARANTEED.
SO WHAT ELSE IS NEW?
YOU'LL "GET HER BACK," AS YOU PUT IT...
... AND SHE'LL BE EXEMPLARY IN THE FIELD, AND THEN, EVENTUALLY...
... YOU'LL ASK HER TO DO NOTHER HORRIBLE BUT OH-SO-NECESSARY THING...
... AND SHE'LL END UP HERE ONCE MORE, AND WE'LL PLAY THIS WHOLE LITTLE DRAMA AGAIN...
... UNTIL THERE'S NOTHING LEFT OF HER FOR YOU TO USE.

6031
CH-KLAK
SHHKK

DAVID'S BOOKS
86 Jan-March
DAVID'S BOOKS
86 March-August
DAVID'S BOOKS
86 March-August
DAVID'S BOOKS
86 March-August
Afghanistan/
Kabul
Taleban
01-07-2001

... AND THE DEJAN BRIEF NEEDS TO BE BACK TO D. INT FIRST THING TOMORROW.
IT'S ON MY DESK?
YES, I PLACED IT UNDER THE ROUTINES.
FINE.
IF THAT'S EVERYTHING...?
YOU'RE FREE.
NO, I'M QUITE DEAR, ACTUALLY.
BUT I'LL BE GOING ALL THE SAME.
HAVE A GOOD NIGHT.
NOT LIKELY.
12
9
3
6

SIR?
WHERE THE *HELL* HAVE YOU BEEN?
I'M SORRY, SIR. I NEEDED TO *VERIFY* SOMETHING.
I THINK I MIGHT HAVE IT, SIR.
MACMILLAN HAD A GIRL, NAME OF CHARLOTTE ALLEN. HE DECLARED HER IN HIS LAST PERSONAL-AND-INTIMATES. SHE WAS CLEARED, LOW-RISK.
HE'D BEEN SENDING HER HIS *NOTEBOOKS* TO HOLD WHEN HE WAS DONE WITH THEM.
HE DID A STORY LATE LAST YEAR, ABOUT HOW THE TALEBAN WAS STILL HOARDING *HEROIN* IN WAREHOUSES ALONG THE PAKISTANI BORDER.
HE HAD A *CONTACT* FOR THE STORY, A MAN NAMED KHALILI FARHADI, NOT A PATHAN.
EXPLAIN.
THE PATHANS ARE THE INDIGENOUS GROUP THAT MAKE UP THE MAJORITY OF THE TALEBAN.
FARHADI WAS LOW-RANKING IN THE GOVERNMENT *BEFORE* THE OUSTER, BUT HE'D BEEN HANGING ON.
HE'D BEEN PASSING INFORMATION TO MACMILLAN FOR HIS STORY.
THEY HAD THEIR *OWN* DROP. NOT ONE OF *OURS*, ONE THAT MACMILLAN SET UP *INDEPENDENTLY*.
I SUPPOSE I SHOULD BE *THANKFUL*.
WHERE'S FARHADI NOW?
THAT'S WHY I'M *LATE*, I HAD TO CONFIRM WITH THE EAST ASIA DESK...

... HE WAS ARRESTED AND EXECUTED TWO WEEKS AGO.
THEY'D HAVE TORTURED FARHADI BEFORE KILLING HIM.
YES, SIR.
DID HE GIVE UP MACMILLAN?
NOT NECESSARILY AS ONE OF OURS, BUT ALMOST CERTAINLY.
WHICH COULD MEAN FARHADI GAVE UP THE DLB, TOO.
MACMILLAN DESCRIBES THE LOCATION IN HERE?
HE WAS OBVIOUSLY AFRAID THE TALEBAN WOULD GET HOLD OF HIS NOTES, SO HE'S VAGUE...
... BUT THERE'S A MOSQUE NEAR THE INTERCONTINENTAL THAT HE REFERS TO, ONLY ABOUT A THOUSAND YARDS FROM THE HOTEL.
MACMILLAN WOULDN'T HAVE SET THE DROP INSIDE THE MOSQUE...
... BUT I WENT DOWN TO THE OPS ROOM AND GOT THIS MAP OF KABUL FROM ALEXIS, AND IF YOU LOOK AT IT...
... YOU SEE THAT THE MOSQUE IS NORTH OF THE HOTEL, ON THE EAST SIDE OF THE STREET...
... WHICH MEA
THE ENTRANCE IS
THE WEST WALL, F
THE STREET, HE
YOU'RE CERTAIN?

IT'S THE WAY THEY'RE CONSTRUCTED, SIR. IN ISLAM, YOU PRAY FACING MECCA.
WHEN IN A MOSQUE, YOU FACE THE WALL THAT FACES MECCA-- IT'S CALLED THE QIBLA WALL. IN KABUL, THAT'S THE EAST.
MACMILLAN WOULD HAVE WANTED TO PROTECT THE DROP, SO IT'S GOT TO BE ON THE NORTHERN OR SOUTHERN SIDE OF THE BUILDING.
WHICH IS IT?
I THINK THE SOUTH, SIR.
IT'S CLOSER TO THE HOTEL, AND WOULD OFFER A LITTLE MORE SHADOW.
IF FARHADI BLEW THE DLB WHEN HE GAVE UP MACMILLAN, AND I ORDER TOM AND ED TO CHECK THE BOX...
... THEY'LL BE WALKING TO THEIR DEATHS.
YOU MIGHT WANT TO HEAD DOWN TO THE OPS ROOM.
YES, SIR.
AND TARA?
SIR?
WELL DONE.
THANK YOU, SIR.
RON? D. OPS. SECURE TO MORNINGSTAR, FIVE MINUTES. I'M COMING DOWN...

YOU THERE!
PARDON ME, CAN YOU HELP?
WE'RE A BIT TURNED AROUND, WE'RE TRYING TO FIND THE ROAD TO KHYBER.
YOU... YOU WANT... KHYBER?
RIGHT, KHYBER. DO YOU KNOW THE WAY?
I CAN... SHOW YOU, YES? SHOW YOU.
ON THE MAP? THAT WOULD BE VERY HELPFUL...

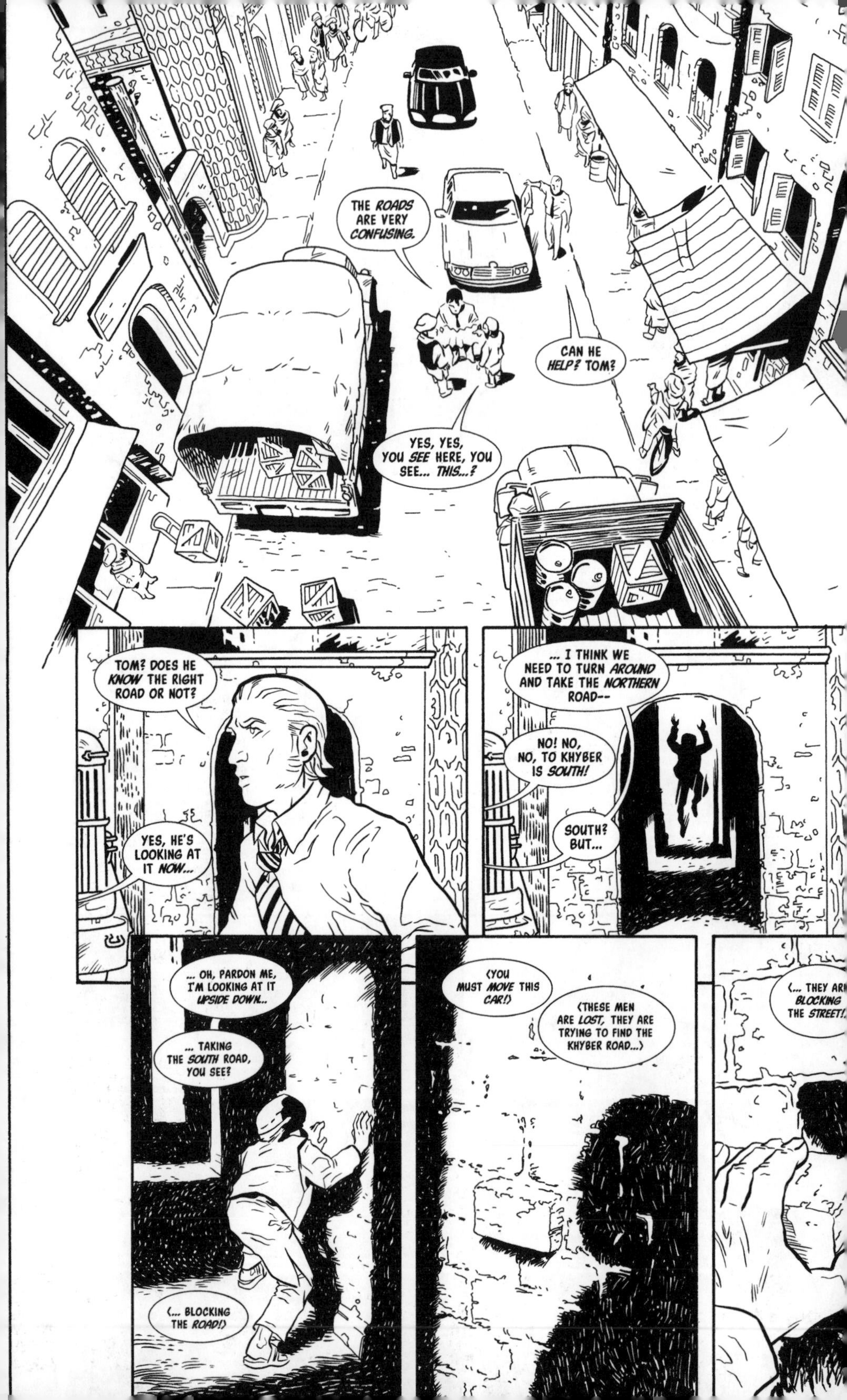
THE ROADS ARE VERY CONFUSING.
CAN HE HELP? TOM?
YES, YES, YOU SEE HERE, YOU SEE... THIS...?
TOM? DOES HE KNOW THE RIGHT ROAD OR NOT?
YES, HE'S LOOKING AT IT NOW...
... I THINK WE NEED TO TURN AROUND AND TAKE THE NORTHERN ROAD--
NO! NO, NO, TO KHYBER IS SOUTH!
SOUTH? BUT...
... OH, PARDON ME, I'M LOOKING AT IT UPSIDE DOWN...
... TAKING THE SOUTH ROAD, YOU SEE?
(... BLOCKING THE ROAD!)
(YOU MUST MOVE THIS CAR!)
(THESE MEN ARE LOST, THEY ARE TRYING TO FIND THE KHYBER ROAD...)
(... THEY AR BLOCKING THE STREET!)

‹WE ARE GIVING THEM DIRECTIONS! JUST WAIT-- ›
‹NO! NO! YOU HAVE THESE-- YOU TELL THESE WESTERNERS THEY MUST MOVE!›
SO IT'S A LEFT HERE, THEN?
THAT'S A RIGHT, TOM.
AH, OOPS. GOT TURNED AROUND AGAIN, IT SEEMS...
YOU CANNOT BE HERE.
YOU ARE BLOCKING THE WAY.
MOVE YOUR CAR NOW...
... OR YOU WILL BE ARRESTED FOR A DISTURBANCE.
NOW SEE HERE. OUR FIRM SPECIALIZES IN IRRIGATION AND WATER RECLAMATION SYSTEMS, AND IF YOU WANT--
EDWARD.
CLEAR THE STREET.
‹CLEAR THE STREET!›
‹YOU! BACK THAT TRUCK UP...›
THANK YOU, THANKS FOR YOUR HELP.

GO.
TELL ME THERE WAS SOMETHING *THERE.*
ED, YOU SHOULD PULL OVER. I'LL NEED TO *DRIVE* US THROUGH THE *BORDER.*

(YOU CAN GO.)
THOUGHT HE WAS GOING TO PULL MY FILLINGS.
THEY LOOK IN THE CLEVER PLACES...
... AND FORGET THE OBVIOUS ONES.
AND THANK GOD FOR THAT.

KABUL
OPERATION: MORNINGSTAR
STATUS: FREE RUN
R.
YES, GO AHEAD.
... YES...
... THATS CONFIRMED?
LET'S HEAR IT.
DELHI STATION, SIR, DELHI NUMBER ONE REPORTING.
TOM, ED, AND THE NUMBER TWO HAVE REACHED PESHAWAR...
KABUL
OPERATION: MORNINGSTAR
STATUS: COMPLETE
... AND THEY HAVE THE LIST.
I'LL INFORM D. OPS RIGHT AWAY.
MCO OUT.
GOOD JOB, EVERYONE.
RON? RING THE FOREIGN OFFICE...
... LET THEM KNOW WE'VE CLEARED KABUL. THEN GET ONTO 'C' AND THE DEPUTY CHIEF, SAME MESSAGE.
NOTIFY D. INT AND THE EAST ASIA DESK...

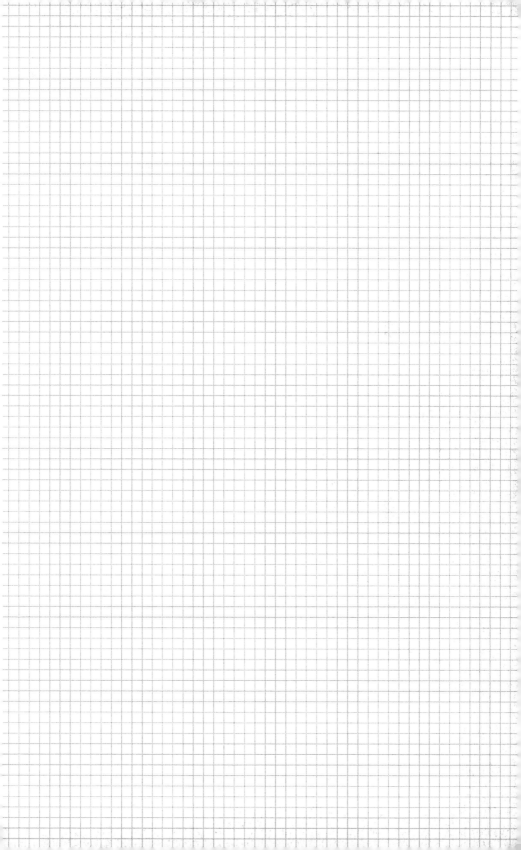

OPERATION: CRYSTAL BALL

WRITTEN BY
GREG RUCKA

ILLUSTRATED BY
LEANDRO FERNANDEZ

LETTERED BY
SEAN KONOT

ORIGINALLY EDITIED BY
JAMIE S. RICH

ROSTER

C—Ubiquitous code-name for the current head of S.I.S.. Real name is Sir Wilson Stanton Davies.

DONALD WELDON—Deputy Chief of Service, has oversight of all aspects of Intelligence gathering and operations. Immediate superior to Crocker.

PAUL CROCKER—Director of Operations, encompassing all field work in all theaters of operations. In addition to commanding individual stations, has direct command of the Special Section–sometimes referred to as Minders –used for special operations.

TOM WALLACE—Head of the Special Section, a Special Operations Officer with the designation Minder One Responsible for the training and continued well-being of his unit, both at home and in the field. Six year veteran of the Minders.

TARA CHACE—Special Operations Officer, designated Minder Two. Entering her third year as Minder.

EDWARD KITTERING—Special Operations Officer, designated Minder Three. Has been with the Special Section for less than a year.

OPS ROOM STAFF

OTHERS

ALEXIS—Mission Control Officer (also called Main Communications Officer)– responsible for maintaining communications between the Operations Room and the agents in the field.

RON—Duty Operations Officer, responsible for monitoring the status and importance of all incoming intelligence, both from foreign stations and other sources.

KATE—Personal Assistant to Paul Crocker, termed P.A. to D.Ops. Possibly the hardest and most important job in the Service.

ANGELA CHANG—CIA Station Chief in London. Has an unofficial intelligence-sharing arrangement with Crocker.

SIMON RAYBURN—Director of Intelligence for S.I.S. (D. Int), essentially Crocker's opposite number. Responsible for the evaluation, interpretation, and dissemination of all acquired intelligence.

DAVID KINNY—Crocker's opposite number at M.I.5, also called the Security Services, with jurisdiction primarily confined to within the U.K.

CHAPTER 1

LONDON.

DREET DREET

MCO OFFICER...

DREET DREET DREET

...TRACKING THE SITUATION --WHAT?--

DUTY OPERATIONS OFFICER, GO AHEAD--

DREET DREET DREET

--JUST A MOMENT--

DREET DREET DREET

MCO, GO AHEAD...

--I'M SORRY, ***WHAT*** DID YOU SAY?

--NEED TO BLOODY ***STOP*** SHOUTING--

...SORRY, JUST A MOMENT...

DREET DREET DREET

...SOMETHING AWFUL'S HAPPENED.

11 SEPTEMBER 2001 1405 HOURS GMT

--C'MON
C'MON MOVE MOVE MOVE!

FOR CHRIST'S SAKE, WALLACE, THE BROAD AND THE BABY ARE LEAVING YOU IN THE DIRT!!

AND YOU TWO, BLOODY SPECIAL SECTION, YOU'RE NOT SPECIAL, YOU'RE JUST SLOW--

--NOW MOVE IT MOVE DAMMIT, LOWER!!

...SHOOTING AT YOU--WOULD THAT KEEP YOUR HEADS DOWN?
AND TO THINK, I LEFT THE REGIMENT FOR THIS.
ADMIT IT, ED, SLOGGING THROUGH MUD TURNS YOU ON.
GOOD FOR THE COMPLEXION, RIGHT?
NOT THAT YOU NEED THE HELP...
..BEING THE MOST BEAUTIFUL BIRD IN THE ENTIRETY OF S.I.S.
RIGHT, BECAUSE SWEAT, MUD, AND SHITE MAKE A GIRL GLOW.
WORKS FOR ME.
AND YOU TALKED THIS WAY TO YOUR MATES IN THE S.A.S., DID YOU?
WOULD HAVE DONE, I SUPPOSE
UFF
--IF I FANCIED ANY OF THEM.
TARA! ED!
INDOORS, NOW.

TARA...
LEAVE IT, TOM.
I'M SUPPOSED TO BE ON THE *RANGE*, ANYWAY.

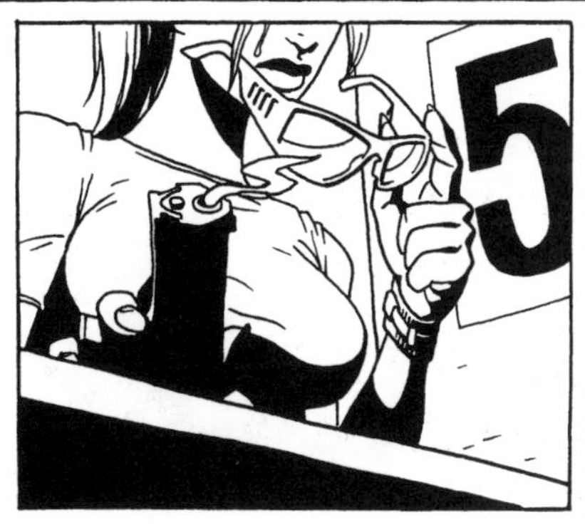

...IN POSITION AND HOLDING.
17 MAY 2002 1529 HOURS GMT
OPERATION: ROSESHORE
STATUS: UNKNOWN
FRANKFURT
WHAT ARE THEY WAITING FOR?
SCHRADER'S UNIT IS COMPLETING THEIR EVACUATION OF THE BLOCK.
THEY'RE TRYING TO DO IT WITHOUT ALERTING THE TARGET.
THEY NEED TO MOVE, PAUL...
...IF THE STAY OUT T MUCH LONG THEY'LL MADE.
LEAST OF THEIR WORRIES, I'D SAY.
WHAT DOES THAT MEAN?
IF IT IS MUGHNIYEH'S BOYS, THERE'LL BE EXPLOSIVE ALL OVER THE PLACE...
...ANY OF THEM BLOWS, YOU'RE LOOKING AT THE LAST OF THE SPECIAL SECTION.
LANGLEY SAID THE LOCATION WAS SAFE--
BUT NOT SAFE ENOUGH TO RISK TASKING ANY OF THE COMPANY'S COVERT ACTION STAFF--
WAIT A SECOND.
IT'S NOT OUR FAULT THAT CHACE AND KITTERING WERE ALREADY IN BERLIN ON BOXKITE WHEN THIS CAME DOWN--
SHUT UP, BOTH OF YOU.

CAN WE TALK TO SCHRADER?
COMS UP AND RUNNING
LANDLINE?
SATLINK.
CONNECT ME.

HE'S IN THE COMMAND POST.
HERR SCHRADER? PAUL CROCKER...
...THEY'RE WITH YOU? GLAD TO HEAR IT. THEN GSG-9 IS *READY*...?
JUST A MOMENT--
--LEX, THEY'VE ESTABLISHED A *LIVE FEED*, SEE IF YOU CAN BRING IT UP.
RIGHT AWAY.
...YES, IT'S COMING IN NOW...YES, I UNDERSTAND...
GOOD LUCK.

IT'S *ON*.

<ENTRY TEAM POSITIONS, STAND-BY...>
<... SWEEP TEAM, STAND-BY... STAND-BY...>
<...ENTRY TEAM... BREACH BREACH *BREACH.*>
<SWEEP TEAM, *MOVE!*>
COMING, ED?
WOULDN'T MISS IT.
5100-EDF

<WE WAIT UNTIL THE *FIRING* STOPS.>
<NO *OBJECTIONS* HERE.>
<ALPHA? SWEEP ONE, SECURE.>
<REPEAT, WE ARE *SECURE.*>
<ALPHA CONFIRMED. COMING *IN.*>
<ALL RIGHT, STAY *CLOSE* UNTIL WE'RE *ALL* THE WAY IN. THERE SHOULDN'T BE ANY *STRAY* GUNS, BUT...>
<OF COURSE.>

<NICE WORK. WELL DONE.>
<THANK YOU, SIR.>

<EVERYONE FINE? GOOD...>

<...LET'S SEE WHAT WE'VE *GOT*...>

THAT WOULD NOT BE MUGHNIYEH?
NO ONE GETS ***THAT*** LUCKY.
THERE'D BE NO WAY TO ***CONFIRM*** IT IF IT WAS, ANYWAY.
THE ISRAELIS SAY HE HAD PLASTIC SURGERY DONE A WHILE BACK. NO IDEA WHAT HE LOOKS LIKE ***NOW.***
A ***VICTORY*** NONETHELESS, WOULDN'T YOU SAY?

WE'LL SEE.
‹HAS THIS BEEN ***CHECKED?***›
‹CHECKED?›

‹FOR ***EXPLOSIVES.***›
‹YES, IT'S ALL ***CLEAR,*** SIR.›
THIS IS WHAT WE WERE ***AFTER.*** I'M TO CARRY IT BACK TO ***LONDON.***

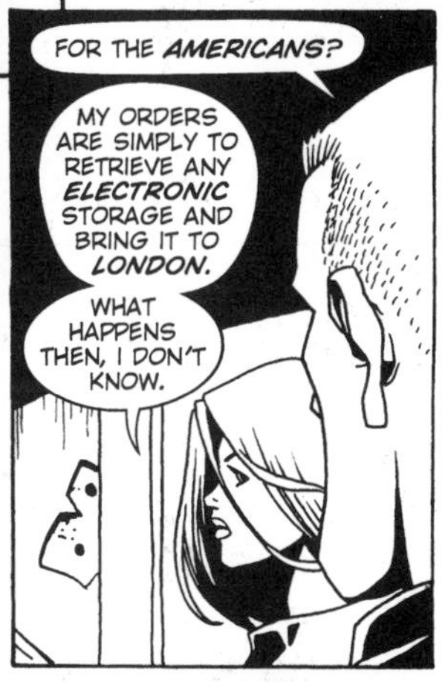

FOR THE ***AMERICANS?***
MY ORDERS ARE SIMPLY TO RETRIEVE ANY ***ELECTRONIC*** STORAGE AND BRING IT TO ***LONDON.***
WHAT HAPPENS THEN, I DON'T KNOW.

THE AMERICANS WILL SHARE THE ***DATA?***
I REALLY CAN'T SAY, MISTER SCHRADER.

VERY WELL. I WILL CALL YOUR MISTER CROCKER AND LET HIM KNOW THAT YOU AND MISTER KITTERING ARE ON YOUR WAY.
THANK YOU.

...FROM DOWNING STREET.

THE PRIME MINISTER WAS PLEASED WITH THE DISPOSITION OF ROSESHORE.
YOU'RE TO PASS THAT ON TO MINDERS TWO AND THREE, PAUL.
YES, SIR.

THE LAPTOP THEY RECOVERED HAS ALREADY GONE TO GROSVENOR SQUARE?
NOT YET.

I WANT US TO LOOK IT OVER FIRST.
PAUL, THIS IS NO TIME TO BE PLAYING GAMES WITH THE C.I.A.
HAVE IT DELIVERED IMMEDIATELY.

THEY CAN WAIT TWENTY-FOUR HOURS.
THE C.I.A. GAVE US ROSESHORE ON THE CONDITION WE HAND OVER ANY DATA--
THEY GAVE IT TO US BECAUSE WE ALREADY HAD TWO AGENTS IN GERMANY AND THEY COULDN'T GET COVERAGE ON THE OP IN TIME.
THEY'LL GET IT AS SOON AS WE'RE DONE.

EXPLAIN YOURSELF, PAUL.

I WANT D. INT TO MAKE A COPY OF THE CONTENTS--
THE C.I.A. WILL DISTRIBUTE THE INFORMATION TO US AFTER THEY PROCESS IT--
BY WHICH YOU MEAN THEY'LL SELECTIVELY EDIT IT FIRST.

SIR.
THE FRANKFURT CELL TIES BACK TO IMAD MUGHNIYEH. MUGHNIYEH IS HEAD OF HIZBULLAH OPERATIONS, WE'VE KNOWN THAT FOR YEARS--
ALL OF WESTERN INTELLIGENCE KNOWS THAT!

DONALD.
LET HIM FINISH.

MUGHNIYEH IS AL-QAEDA --CLOSE TIES TO BIN LADEN'S *SUCCESSOR*, AYMAN *AL ZAWAHIRI*.
BOTH MEN HANDLE *PLANNING* AND *OPERATIONS*, WHICH MEANS THEY HAVE ACCESS TO FUND DISBURSEMENT.

IRAQ HAS BEEN PROVIDING AL-QAEDA MONEY AND SUPPORT VIA THE S.S.O. FOR ALMOST *TEN* YEARS.
IF THE FRANKFURT CELL REALLY *WAS* ONE OF MUGHNIEYH'S THEN THE *MONEY* COULD LEAD *BACK* TO THE *S.S.O.*
THIS IS OUR CHANCE TO *CHOKE OFF* THE SUPPLY AND *STARVE* THE WHOLE *NETWORK*.

THE S.S.O., ONE OF HUSSEIN'S SONS HEADS IT UP?
QUSAI HUSSEIN, YES, SIR.
THE AMERICANS *KNOW* ALL OF THIS, PAUL.
WHY THE SUDDEN *RETICENCE* TO SHARE WITH THEM?

MUGHNIYEH ORCHESTRATED THE *KIDNAPPING* OF THE C.I.A.'S BEIRUT STATION CHIEF IN *'84*.
WILLIAM BUCKLEY, SIR. IT TRIGGERED THE 'IRANGATE' SCANDAL. ARMS TO IRAN TO FACILITATE THE RELEASE OF BUCKLEY.
IT *FAILED*. BUCKLEY WAS *EXECUTED*.

BUT ALL OF THIS *MAY* BE BESIDE THE *POINT*. IT'S ALSO AN ISSUE OF *TIME*.
THE LAPTOP MUST GO TO LANGLEY FOR *EXTRACTION* AND *ANALYSIS*...

...DATA THEN DISSEMINATED TO THE N.S.A. AND THE D.I.A., THROUGHOUT THEIR MILITARY INTELLIGENCE AND THEIR OFFICE OF HOMELAND SECURITY...
...TO THE F.B.I., THE D.E.A., THE A.T.F., THE I.R.S., AND *THEN* TO THE *ALLIES*...

...IT'LL BE *NEXT* BOXING DAY BEFORE WE SEE THE *ABSTRACT*.
THIS WAY, WE'RE IN THE *GAME* EARLY, AND WE CAN PROVIDE ENHANCED *SUPPORT* TO THE *ALLIED* OPERATION.

AND WE CAN *PURSUE* THE FINANCIAL LEADS WHILE THE C.I.A. PURSUES MUGHNIYEH.
THERE IS *THAT*, AS WELL.

CHENG HAS *APPROVED* YOU DOING THIS?
NO...

...BUT SHE *OWES* ME.

...MOTHERFUCKER!
GIVE THAT TO ME NOW OR I SWEAR TO GOD I'LL AUTHORIZE A COVERT ON YOUR PASTY ASS!
THAT'S UNCALLED FOR, ANGELA.
I'M NATURALLY FAIR-SKINNED.
SHUT UP.
LINDSEY? COURIER PACK, IMMEDIATE TO LANGLEY.
RIGHT AWAY.
SEND IT OUT NOW.
WILL DO.
YOU ARE INCLUDED ON THE CIRCULATION LIST, YOU KNOW. YOU'D HAVE SEEN IT EVENTUALLY.
I WANTED THE UNEXPURGATED VERSION.
DON'T WE ALL?
RAYBURN'S PEOPLE ARE GOING OVER IT?
THEY STARTED LAST NIGHT.

IF WE PULL A LEAD ON MUGHNIYEH, CAN YOU GIVE ME OPS SUPPORT?
IT'LL DEPEND ON WHAT YOU'RE AFTER.
I'D WANT THE MINDERS.
IT'D HAVE TO GET PAST WELDON BEFORE C COULD APPROVE IT.

I'D MAKE IT WORTH YOUR TIME. JUST ABOUT ANYTHING FROM THE COMPANY STORE.
SHOULDN'T BE A HARD SELL. ANYTHING THAT CONTINUES TO LINK THE IRAQIS WITH--
FUCK THE IRAQIS.

THIS IS ABOUT BEIRUT.
IT WAS NEVER CONFIRMED THAT MUGHNIYEH DID ANYTHING OTHER THAN AUTHORIZE THE SNATCH.
BULLSHIT. IT WAS MUGHNIYEH WHO KIDNAPPED, TORTURED, AND THEN MURDERED BUCKLEY.
JESUS, PAUL. I'VE READ THE FUCKING REPORTS...

...THAT TERRORIST COCKSUCKER KILLED OUR MAN WITH HIS OWN HANDS.
IF BUCKLEY HAD BEEN S.I.S., YOU'D WANT THE SAME THING.

NATO CAN BLOW-UP ALL THE CAMPS THEY WANT, THEY CAN PUT ALL OF AL-QAEDA ON TRIAL, I DON'T CARE...

CENTRAL INTELLIGENCE AGENCY
UNITED STATES OF AMERICA
...THE COMPANY IS GOING TO SETTLE THINGS WITH MUGHNIYEH ONCE AND FOR ALL.

CAIRO.
STATE YOUR BUSINESS.
I DO NOT... UH...NOT GOOD ENGLISH? YOU... FOR VISA?
APPLICATION HOURS ARE OVER.
NO, NO, NOT... PARLEZ-VOUS FRANCAIS?
...NO...WHAT? I...PLEASE, MY ENGLISH...
I'M SORRY, SIR. YOU'LL HAVE BETTER LUCK TOMORROW.
I DON'T... JE M'APPELLE MAHMOUD YOUSSEF...
...S'IL VOUS PLAIT, IL FAUT QUE JE PARLE AVEC VOTRE AMBASSADEUR...
...C'EST UNE URGENCE...
I AM BEING WATCHED.
I MUST SPEAK TO
AMBASSADOR.
INFORMATION
UK CITIZEN

I'M TRYING TO *WORK,* HERE.

IF YOU'RE SAYING THAT YOU'D RATHER A MAN LIKE MUGHNIYEH TO *ME,* I'LL SOB.

AND IF I SAID I'D RATHER THE *TEA LADY* TO YOU, *THEN* WHAT?

I'D SAY THERE'S *HOPE* BECAUSE IT'D MEAN YOU WERE *LYING.* I WOULD SAY A *FLAME* OF *POTENTIAL* NOW BURNS--

WHAT MOVIE?

--AND THAT I WOULD *SHIELD* THAT *FLAME...*

...YOU, UH... WHAT?

CAIRO
...SOONEST FLIGHT?
DONE, SIR.
B.A. ONE-FIVE-FIVE DEPARTS HEATHROW SEVENTEEN HUNDRED HOURS, ARRIVES *CAIRO* TWENTY-THREE FIFTY-FIVE *LOCAL.*

DO IT, *ONE* SEAT.
18 MAY 2002 1449 HOURS GMT
MINDER TWO TO *BRIEF* AND *GO.*

WHERE AM I GOING?
CAIRO.
WE'VE HAD A *WALK-IN...*
DUTY OPERATIONS OFFICER, ONE SEAT, MINDER TWO, B.A. FLIGHT ONE-FIVE-FIVE...

...A LEBANESE NATIONAL NAMED MAHMOUD YOUSSEF JUST *DROPPED* INTO THEIR LAPS.
HARD-APPROACH, RIGHT AT THE *GATES,* BUT PASSED THE *WORD* IN WRITING, SO IF IT'S *LEGIT,* HE MAY STILL BE *SECURE.*
WHAT'S HE *DO?*
CLAIMS HE'S A *SOLDIER* IN THE GROUPE ISLAMIQUE ARMÉ...

...WHICH COULD TIE HIM TO EGYPTIAN ISLAMIC JIHAD *AND* HIZBULLAH, MAYBE EVEN KNOWLEDGE OF OPERATIONS IN THE *BEKA'A* VALLEY.
G.I.A. IS IN THE *WEST.* IF MISTER YOUSSEF CAME DOWN FROM PARIS, HIS *MATES* KNOW HE'S GONE *MISSING.*

IE SAYS HE WAS IN CAIRO TO ***LIASON*** WITH E.I.J. OPERATIONS,
ND IS CLAIMING TO HAVE ***KNOWLEDGE*** OF A PENDING
ETALIATORY STRIKE FOR THE S.A.S. ACTION IN KANDAHAR.
ON THE LEVEL?
COULD BE. CHECK THE ***STORY*** FIRST...

...AND IF IT ***OLDS,*** SEE IF YOU CAN ***BOOMERANG*** HIM.
WE DO THIS ***QUICKLY,*** WE COULD WIN OURSELVES A MAN ON THE ***INSIDE.***
RIGHT.

FLUENT IN ***FRENCH?***
YES, BUT HIS ***ENGLISH*** IS ***SPOTTY.*** THAT'S WHY ***YOU'RE*** GOING.
HE'S AT THE EMBASSY ***NOW?***
THEY'RE KEEPING HIM UNDER WRAPS UNTIL YOU FINISH THE ***INTERVIEW.***

SEEMS STRAIGHT FORWARD ENOUGH.
GOOD. FINISH UP HERE AND ***GO.***
I'LL ADVISE THE DEPUTY CHIEF.

EXCUSE ME, SIR?
LATER, ED.

CAN I HAVE A *MINUTE,* SIR?
PAUL. COME IN.

I'M SENDING MINDER TWO TO CAIRO. WE'VE HAD A WALK-IN, COULD BE A LEAD INTO AL-QAEDA.
YOU DON'T SOUND ***CONVINCED.***
THERE'S A ***FIRST*** TIME FOR EVERYTHING, SIR.

THE *TIMING* BOTHERS ME.
TOO SOON AFTER THE ACTION WITH GSG-9, YOU MEAN?
YES, SIR.
WHAT'S THIS WALK-IN OFFERING?

HE'S SAYING THAT THE EIJ IS MOVING AGAINST BRITISH INTERESTS IN THE WAKE OF KANDAHAR.
THE E.I.J.? THEY HAVEN'T MOVED IN ***EUROPE*** SINCE THE LATE '80S. IS IT ***LIKELY*** HE'S TELLING THE ***TRUTH?***
NO.
BUT EVEN ***IF*** HE'S ***NOT*** ON THE ***LEVEL,*** WE'RE OBLIGATED TO ***ACT.***
I AGREE.

WHY AREN'T YOU BRIEFING MINDER TWO?
SHE'S A BRIGHT GIRL, BOSS. I ONLY HAD TO GO THROUGH IT ONCE.

SHE'S ON HER WAY OUT TO HEATHROW NOW.
THEN WHY ARE YOU HERE INSTEAD OF THE PIT?
KITTERING HAS A CONCERN, AND I SHARE IT--
KITTERING HAS A CRUSH, AND NEEDS TO KEEP IT IN CHECK.

THAT'S AS MAY BE. THIS COULD BE A SET-UP.
I HAD THOUGHT OF THAT, TOM.

SHE KNOWS I'M NOT SENDING HER OUT THERE ON HOLIDAY.
SHE'LL EVALUATE YOUSSEF'S WORTH AND TAKE IT FROM THERE.
YES, BUT YOUSSEF CAN PROMISE US ANYTHING, CAN'T HE?
YOU SAID IT YOURSELF. SHE'S A BRIGHT GIRL.

WE'LL JUST HAVE TO WAIT AND SEE, TOM.

MY NAME'S CHACE.
COLIN HODGSON IS EXPECTING ME.
JUST A MOMENT, MISS CHACE.
YES, SIR, NAME OF CHACE.
YES.
VERY GOOD, SIR.
SORRY ABOUT THAT, MISS CHACE.
THEY'RE WAITING FOR YOU INSIDE.

MISS CHACE?
COLIN HODGSON, SECOND DEFENCE ATTACHÉ.
PLEASURE TO MEET YOU.
I'M SURE. IF YOU'LL FOLLOW ME, WE HAVE HIM WAITING IN THE DEFENCE WING.
THIS IS VERY UNUSUAL FOR US, WE HAVEN'T HAD ANYTHING LIKE THIS HERE FOR YEARS, NOW.
WE'LL ALL BE MORE THAN A LITTLE RELIEVED TO HAVE YOU BOTH OUT OF OUR HAIR.
MISTER HODGSON.
YES? WHAT IS IT?
THIS WILL TAKE EXACTLY AS LONG AS IT WILL TAKE, NO LESS.
IF A MINDER IN YOUR EMBASSY MAKES YOU NERVOUS, THEN YOU'D BEST GET OVER IT, AND SOON.
I BEG YOUR PARDON?
YOU SHOULD KNOW, MISS CHACE...
...DONALD WELDON AND I WERE AT SCHOOL TOGETHER.
BULLY FOR YOU.

<YES... YES, I...>

<I KNOW OF A PLOT, YOU SEE...>

<...A CHEMICAL PLOT....>

GREG RUCKA
LEO FERNANDEZ

CHAPTER 2

LEANDRO FERNANDEZ

"RELIABILITY, YOU SEE? THAT'S ALWAYS BEEN THE PROBLEM WITH CHEMICAL AND BIOLOGICAL AGENTS.
AL-HARTUM 11 Km
KASSALA 400 Km
"UNLESS THEY HAVE BEEN WEAPONIZED, THEY ARE REMARKABLY UNSTABLE. DIFFICULT TO TRANSPORT, DIFFICULT TO VECTOR.
Construction Quadrat
"AS A RESULT, THEY ARE ALSO DIFFICULT TO MANUFACTURE...
.NOT ON A
MALL SCALE,
T RATHER ON
LARGE ONE.
"THAT'S WHY SO MANY ORGANIZATIONS HAVE ESCHEWED THEIR USE. TOO MUCH EFFORT, NOT ENOUGH RESULT.
"THE ESSENCE OF TERROR BEING TO ENGENDER THE MAXIMUM HORROR WITH THE LEAST EFFORT.
Construction Quadrat
"OTHER PROBLEMS EXIST IN THE PRODUCTION, AS WELL. FUNDING IS CRITICAL, AS WELL AS THE PROPER ENVIRONMENT...
"...AND WHILE THE REQUISITE EQUIPMENT CAN BE ACQUIRED WITH EASE--RELATIVELY SPEAKING --IT IS FAR HARDER TO FIND PEOPLE TRAINED TO DO THE NECESSARY WORK.
"IT REQUIRES THE RAREST COMBINATION OF ZEALOTRY AND BRILLIANCE..."

<...WITHOUT THAT CRITICAL COMPONENT, MISS CHACE, ONE IS CONFINED TO PLAYING ON THE SMALLEST OF PITCHES.>

<YOU'VE SUCCEEDED IN HOLDING MY ATTENTION, MISTER YOUSSEF.>

<BUT THUS FAR, YOU'VE CONFINED YOURSELF TO THE HYPOTHETICAL.>

<YOUR NOTE SAID YOU HAD KNOWLEDGE OF AN ACTUAL PLOT IN THE OFFING.>

<YES... YES, THAT IS TRUE...>

<...I WAS RECRUITED INTO THE G.I.A. THREE YEARS AGO...AS A STUDENT, IN PARIS.>

<MOSTLY I JOINED BECAUSE OF MY OUTRAGE AT THE TREATMENT OF MY PEOPLE BY THE ZIONISTS...>

<...BUT ALSO BECAUSE I WAS A ROMANTIC.>

<AND YOU'VE FOUND ROMANCE OVERRATED?>

<IT WOULD BE BETTER TO SAY THAT, IN THE LAST YEAR, I HAV BECOME MORE PRAGMATIC.>

‹I'M NOT CERTAIN YOU COULD GIVE US ANYTHING WORTH THAT MUCH, MISTER YOUSSEF. PERHAPS A MORE REASONABLE SUM IS IN ORDER?›

‹AND IF I TOLD YOU THAT THE EGYPTIAN ISLAMIC JYHAD NOT ONLY HAS ACQUIRED A LARGE QUANTITY OF SARIN GAS...›
‹...BUT ALSO HAS DEVELOPED A DELIVERY SYSTEM THAT WILL GUARANTEE CASUALTIES IN THE TENS OF THOUSANDS...›
‹...AND HAS PICKED A TARGET TO BE HIT IN THE NEXT EIGHT WEEKS...›

‹...WOULD THAT JUSTIFY THE PRICE?›
‹IT MIGHT.›
‹BUT IT WOULD TAKE MORE THAN JUST YOUR GOOD WORD.›

‹ONLY FAIR.›
‹I MUST RETURN TO PARIS THIS MORNING, OR ELSE MY BROTHERS IN THE G.I.A. WILL WONDER WHERE I'VE GONE.›
‹I'LL BE IN ROME TWO WEEKS FROM TUESDAY, AT THE BARBERINI, UNDER THE NAME RAHEDI.›

‹THAT SHOULD GIVE YOU ENOUGH TIME TO VERIFY THESE COORDINATES.›
‹THE, UH... SECOND SET OF NUMBERS IS FOR MY SWISS ACCOUNT.›

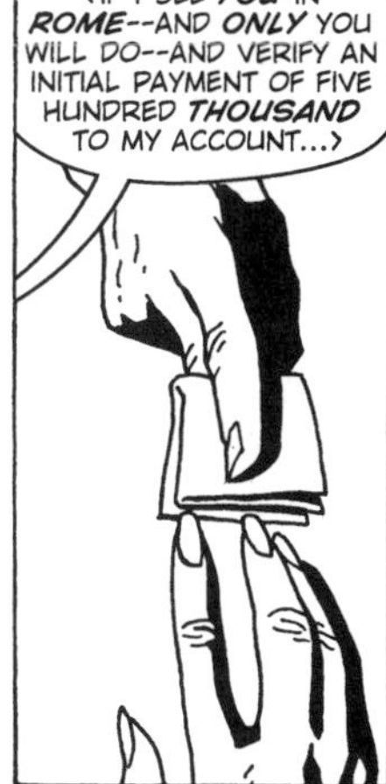
‹IF I SEE YOU IN ROME--AND ONLY YOU WILL DO--AND VERIFY AN INITIAL PAYMENT OF FIVE HUNDRED THOUSAND TO MY ACCOUNT...›

‹...I'LL ASSUME YOU'RE TAKING ME SERIOUSLY.›

CHACE! MISS CHACE!

ARE YOU *QUITE* FINISHED HERE?
THE *TWO* OF YOU WERE *AT* IT ALL *NIGHT*. THIS IS AN *EMBASSY*, NOT SOME *SOCIAL*--

...CLUB.

I REQUIRE THE *USE* OF YOUR *COMMUNICATION* ROOM.

WHAT? WHY?

THAT IS *NONE* OF YOUR CONCERN, MISTER HODGSON.

COMMUNICAT

IT BLOODY WELL *IS* MY CONCERN!

I'VE AN EMBASSY TO *PROTECT* HERE!

COMMUNICATIONS

I'M NOT ABOUT TO HAVE ONE OF PAUL CROCKER'S *GUNSLINGERS* MAKING *MESSES* IN MY FRONT YARD!

MISTER HODGSON...

...I AM AN **OFFICER** OF THE **S.I.S.**, AND I REQUIRE YOUR **COOPERATION.**

YOU'RE A **MINDER** WHO JUST **SPENT** THE **NIGHT** WITH A SUSPECTED **TERRORIST** UNDER MY **ROOF.**

EITHER YOU **MOVE** RIGHT **NOW,** OR I SHALL MOVE **YOU...**

...AND I SHALL DO IT IN SUCH A **WAY** AS TO MAKE YOUR **FUTURE** A VERY **HIGH-PITCHED** ONE.

COMMUNICATIONS

23 MAY
2002
0817 HOURS
GMT
...RIGHT, READ THEM AGAIN...
...HMM... SOMEWHERE IN THE SAHARA I'D EXPECT.
NO, I SHOULDN'T THINK SO...
...THOUGH IT IS INTERESTING THAT HE VOLUNTEERED TO GO BACK HIMSELF...
...YES...WELL, GREED OBVIOUSLY IS PART OF IT.
WE'LL DISCUSS IT WHEN YOU'RE BACK HERE. ANYTHING ELSE?
...I SEE. WHAT'S HIS NAME?
15:50:12N
32:11:98E
...NO, DON'T KNOW HIM...MUST HAVE BEEN APPOINTED AFTER I WAS IN THE FIELD...
...YES, WELL, I WOULDN'T WORRY ABOUT IT TOO MUCH.
COME ON HOME.
SEE YOU TOMORROW.

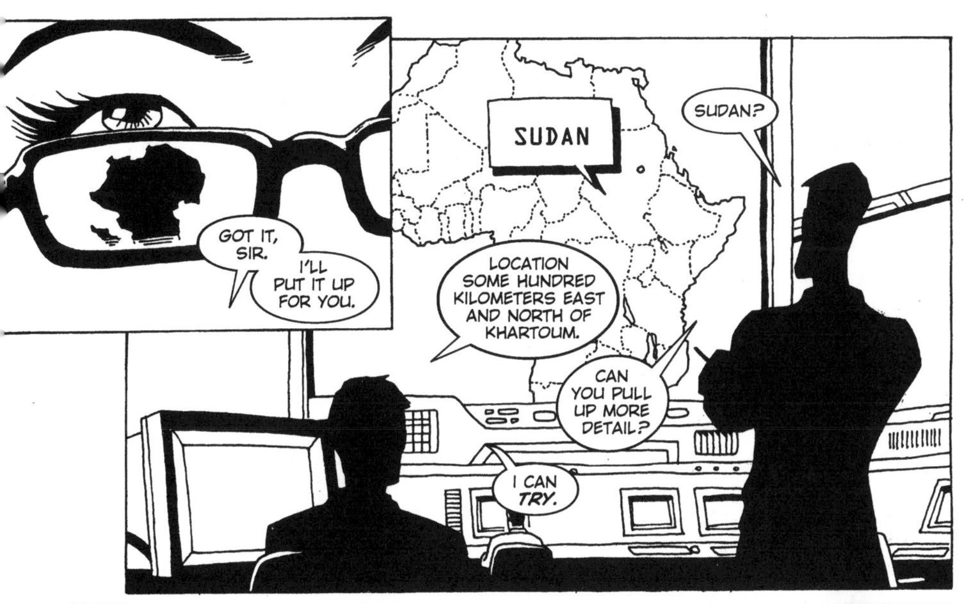
GOT IT, SIR.
I'LL PUT IT UP FOR YOU.
SUDAN
SUDAN?
LOCATION SOME HUNDRED KILOMETERS EAST AND NORTH OF KHARTOUM.
CAN YOU PULL UP MORE DETAIL?
I CAN *TRY.*

YES, LEX, IF IT WOULDN'T BE *TOO* MUCH *BOTHER.*

THAT'S THE *BEST* WE'VE GOT.
Khartoum

WORSE THAN *NOTHING.*
THE *AMERICANS* MIGHT HAVE SOMETHING.
UNDOUBTEDLY.

BEATS ME, LOVE.

KATE? JUMP ON THE NORTH AFRICA DESK FOR ME...
...ANYTHING THEY HAVE ON THE AREA WEST OF KHARTOUM.
YES, SIR.
DEPUTY CHIEF IS WAITING IN YOUR OFFICE.
GOOD MORNING, SIR.
PAUL. EVERYTHING STEADY IN THE OPS ROOM?
MINDER TWO'S COMPLETED HER EVALUATION.

SHE'LL BE BACK TOMORROW. I'LL DEBRIEF HER THEN.
I SEE.

I'M SORRY, SIR, WAS THERE SOMETHING ELSE?
YES, THERE WAS.

I WAS CLEARING THE IMMEDIATES FROM MY DESK THIS MORNING WHEN COLIN HODGSON CALLED ME FROM CAIRO.
YOU KNOW WHO HE IS, OF COURSE.
CAIRO EMBASSY. SECOND DEFENCE ATTACHÉ.
MINDER TWO LIAISED WITH HIM UPON HER ARRIVAL.
YES.
HE CLAIMS SHE THREATENED HIS LIFE THIS MORNING.
THAT'S ABSURD.
YOU'RE CALLING COLIN HODGSON A LIAR?
I'M SAYING HE'S OVERREACTING TO AN ARGUMENT THEY HAD ABOUT ACCESS TO THE EMBASSY'S COMS ROOM.
CHACE TOLD ME ABOUT IT WHEN SHE REPORTED IN. HE WAS RETICENT TO GRANT HER ACCESS.
YET SHE CALLED IN JUST THE SAME.
EMBASSY STAFF IS OBLIGATED TO GRANT COMS TO ANY MINDER IN THEIR THEATRE OF OPERATION.
THAT'S A STANDING ORDER, YOU KNOW IT AS WELL AS I.
YES, THEY ARE.
DON'T WORRY, PAUL...
...IT'S PROBABLY NOTHING.
SIR? NOTHING FROM THE NORTH AFRICA DESK. SHOULD I ASK D. INT TO COME BY?
YES.
THANK YOU, KATE.

CHRIST, ED.
WOULD YOU AND HER DESK LIKE TO BE ALONE?
JUST THINKING.
YES, AND I KNOW JUST WHAT YOU WERE THINKING ABOUT, TOO.

YOU'RE A DIRTY OLD MAN, TOM.

I'M NOT THE ONE WITH DROOL STAINS ALL DOWN MY FRONT.

CAN I HELP IT IF I'M KEEN ON HER?
YOU CAN TRY NOT TO BE SO OBVIOUS ABOUT IT, ED.
THERE'S NO REG SAYS I CAN'T TAKE HER OUT FOR A DRINK AND A SHOW.

NO. BUT D. OPS WON'T LIKE IT--
SOD D. OPS.

--AND I CAN'T SAY I'M TOO PLEASED, EITHER.

JUST...GO CAREFULLY.
WE'RE NOT IN A SETTLE-AND-RAISE-A-BROOD KIND OF BUSINESS.

SIMON.
D. INT, SIR.
PAUL. I UNDERSTAND YOU HAVE SOME QUESTIONS ABOUT *SUDAN?*
YES. LOOKING FOR ANYTHING ON INSTALLATIONS WEST OF KHARTOUM.
YOU MUST BE *JOKING...*
...WE HAVEN'T HAD RELIABLE *INTEL* FROM THE REGION FOR *TWENTY* YEARS.
I'M *NOT* EVEN CERTAIN IF WE HAVE ANY *AGENTS* THERE AT ALL.
RABAK AL-HATAWAH, BUT HE'S IN *KUSTI,* AND *PASSIVE* OPS *ONLY.*
MUST BE *BORED* OUT OF HIS *MIND.*
KATE? CALL CHENG AT GROSVENOR SQUARE, TELL HER I WANT TO SEE HER THIS AFTERNOON.

YES, MASTER.
C.I.A. WON'T HAVE ANYONE ON THE GROUND, EITHER, PAUL.
THEY'VE RELIED ON *ELINT* IN THE REGION SINCE '88.

WHAT DID YOUSSEF TELL CHACE?
CLAIMS THAT THE E.I.J. HAS ACQUIRED OR MANUFACTURED A QUANTITY OF SARIN ALONG WITH A HIGH-YIELD DELIVERY SYSTEM FOR THE GAS...

...AND HAS PICKED A TARGET FULL OF U.K. NATIONALS TO BE HIT IN THE NEXT EIGHT WEEKS.
ANY OF THIS VERIFIED?
THAT'S WHAT I WAS HOPING YOU COULD DO.

AL-QA'EDA HAS EXTENSIVE HOLDINGS IN SUDAN, SET-UP EITHER BY BIN-LADEN OR HIS ASSOCIATES...
...ZIRQANI, ALTHEMAR AL MUBARAKA, BAREBA, AL HIJRA CONSTRUCTION...

...EVEN AN AG FACILITY IN KASALLA WHICH DEVELOPS HYBRIDS FOR COMMERCIAL AND OTHER AGRICULTURAL PRODUCE.
ANY OF THOSE COULD FRONT A C.B.W. OPERATION.
BUT NO PROOF.
NEVER VERIFIED. DIDN'T YOUSSEF PROVIDE CHACE WITH ANYTHING?

HE WANTS TWO MILLION POUNDS BEFORE HE SAYS MORE.
SIR? ANGELA CHENG CAN MEET YOU IN THE PARK IN FORTY MINUTES.

THANKS, KATE.
I'LL LEAVE YOU TO IT, THEN.

...PROMISING DATA OFF THE *LAPTOP.*
THAT'S NOT ACTUALLY WHAT I WANTED TO MEET YOU ABOUT.
NO? THIS ABOU MINDER TWO QUICK TRIP CAIRO?
...I WON'T ASK *HOW* YOU KNOW ABOUT THAT.
PROBABLY JUST AS WE
C.I.A. DOESN'T HAVE ANYONE ON THE GROUND IN SUDAN, DO THEY?
ARE YOU *MAD?*
WE TRIED TO GET A *STATION* SET UP IN SUR SUDAN YEAR BEFORE LAST...
...NEARLY GOT OUR MAN *DUNKED* IN THE RED SEA.
WHY?
LONDON BOY
...BUT LANGLEY WILL WANT TO KNOW WHAT THEY GET IN *TRADE.*
THINK OF IT AS A *RETURN* FOR OUR HELP IN FRANKFURT.
DOG WASTE ONLY
NOT SURE THAT'LL *BUY* MUCH, PAUL.
THEY THINK OF FRANKFURT AS CONTINUED *ALLIED* SUPPORT IN THE *WAR* ON *TERROR.*
THA
POLIT
THAT'S
OUR

LET'S WALK.

CAN YOU GET ME *KEYHOLE* IMAGERY FOR THESE *COORDINATES?*

I *COULD...*

LD YOU
TEN TO
RSELF?

OUR END *IS* POLITICAL.
YOU KNOW WHAT I MEAN.

I'LL SEE WHAT I CAN DO.

30 MAY
2002
0903 HOURS
GMT
...COFFEE IN THE *PIT?*
WE *WOULD,* BUT WALLACE KEEPS FORGETTING TO BUY *MORE.*
BESIDES, LEX, YOU MAKE A *BETTER* POT.
ANYTHING FROM THE AMERICANS YET?
NO. RON THINKS THEY'RE *DRAGGING* THEIR *HEELS.*
IT'S BEEN OVER A *WEEK.*
TARA. MORNING.

MISTER KITTERING, GOOD MORNING.
HAVE A PLEASANT NIGHT, THEN?

VERY *QUIET,* THANK YOU.
TALK TO YOU LATER, LEX.

TARA, HOLD UP!
WALK FASTER.

YOU'RE GOING TO KEEP MAKING ME CHASE YOU?
KEEPS YOU FIT, DOESN'T IT?
YOU'D AGREED TO A MOVIE A WHILE BACK, IF YOU RECALL.

SPECIAL OPERATIONS
Wallace, T. Head of Section
Chace, T.
Kittering, E.
HAD I?
ALL I RECALL DOING WAS ASKING WHAT MOVIE YOU HAD IN MIND.

THE PIT
YOU'RE LEADING ME ON, THAT'S WHAT YOU'RE DOING.

I'VE GIVEN THIS SOME THOUGHT, ED.
OH YES?
YES...

...AND I'VE DECIDED YOU DESPERATELY NEED A HOBBY.

WELL, YOU'VE GOT THE DESPERATION PART RIGHT, BUT WHAT I NEED--
TARA--

--HAVE YOU CLEARED THE ROUTINES YET?
NOT YET. JUST GOT IN.
D. INT WANTS YOU TO REVIEW THE SIGNAL FROM MARSEILLE.

I'LL GET RIGHT ON IT.

IS THAT CHENG?
LOOKS LIKE. HELLO, MA'AM.
KATE.

C'MON IN.

YOU'VE BEEN KEEPING ME WAITING. I HOPE IT'S WORTH IT.
NOT SO FAST.

LANGLEY DIDN'T GO FOR THE "HELPED-IN-FRANKFURT" ANGLE.
THEY WANT MORE.
IT'S BEEN A BLOODY WEEK, ANGELA! THEY COULDN'T HAVE COME BACK SOONER?

WE DO HAVE PROBLEMS OF OUR OWN, YOU KNOW.
FOR MORE I GET WHAT?
A KEYHOLE WILL BE RE-ROUTED TO THE SUDAN. INFRARED, HIGH-FOCUS, THE WHOLE DEAL.
YOU'LL BE ABLE TO COUNT ZITS ON WHOEVER IS THERE.

THERE IS A TIME CONCERN ON THIS, ANGELA.
YOU'LL HAVE THE PICTURES BY MONDAY.
AND IN EXCHANGE?

RECOGNIZE HIM?

SHOULD I?
TECHNICALLY, YES. BUT THERE'S NO WAY YOU COULD.

THAT'S MUGNIYEH. THE S.V.R. SNAPPED THAT OF HIM IN TABRIZ, EN ROUTE TO IRAQ.
HOW'D THEY GET IT?

DUMB LUCK. HE'D MET WITH AN IRAQI S.S.O. OFFICER THEY'D HAD UNDER SURVEILLANCE, THEY DIDN'T KNOW WHO THE HELL HE WAS.
THE S.V.R AGENT ON THE TAIL WENT BACK INTO THE CAFÉ THEY'D EATEN AT, BRIBED THE WAITER AND TOOK THE DISHES.
THEY RAN THE PRINTS. HIRTEEN-POINT MATCH.
THAT'S THE COCKSUCKER WHO KILLED OUR GUY.
YOU KNOW WHAT I WANT.
YOU'RE OUT OF YOUR MIND, ANGELA.
IT'S OUR PRICE.
I'LL NEVER GET CLEARANCE TO PUT A MINDER INTO IRAQ.
THEN DO WITHOUT IT. KITTERING'S EX-S.A.S., HE COULD HANDLE THE DROP.
VISITOR
WHERE IS HE SUPPOSED TO GO? ASSUMING THIS IS MUGNIYEH, YOU'RE NOT TELLING ME THE S.V.R. GOT HIS ITINERARY?
READ IT YOURSELF...
TOP SECRET
...THE S.V.R. HAD THE CAFÉ WIRED.

WHY ISN'T THE COMPANY'S COVERT ACTION STAFF ON THIS?
LANGLEY DOESN'T WANT THE EXPOSURE.
BUT THEY DON'T MIND IT FALLING TO US?
AS I SAID, PAUL. THAT'S THE PRICE.
RE-ROUTE YOUR DAMN KEYHOLE.
I'LL SEE WHAT I CAN DO ABOUT MUGNIYEH.
IT'S GOT TO HAPPEN SOON.
SO NOW YOU KNOW HOW I FEEL.
KATE'LL SHOW YOU OUT.

DREET
DREET

MINDER ONE...
...NOTHING I CAN'T PUT DOWN. I'LL BE RIGHT *UP*.

YOU ON YOUR *BIKE*, THEN?
D. OPS WANTS ME IN HIS *OFFICE* BEFORE I HEAD *HOME* FOR THE NIGHT.
OOOH, HAVE YOU BEEN *NAUGHTY*, TOM?

NOT NEARLY *ENOUGH*.
SEE YOU TWO TOMORROW.

FANCY AN EARLY *DINNER?*

YOU *BUY*.

--CAN'T BE SERIOUS ABOUT THIS!
I MEAN, IF IT'S THAT IMPORTANT, WHY AREN'T THEY HANDLING IT THEMSELVES?
CHENG CLAIMS THEY CAN'T PLACE ANYONE IN TIME.
IT COULD ACCOUNT FOR THE DELAY IN LANGLEY GETTING BACK TO US, TOM.

YOU'VE GOT HER WORD THAT IT'S MUGNIYEH, THAT'S IT.
THE WHOLE S.V.R. ANGLE COULD BE UTTER CRAP!
YOU THINK I HAVEN'T CONSIDERED THAT?

ACCORDING TO WHAT YOUSSEF TOLD CHACE, THE E.I.J. HAS A TARGET PICKED SOMEPLACE IN THE NEXT MONTH AND A HALF.
WE'VE GOT LESS THAN A WEEK TO DETERMINE IF HE'S ON THE LEVEL, TOM.

WE NEED THE AMERICANS. I DON'T SEE ANOTHER WAY.
YOU'LL BE DOWN TO TWO MINDERS, YOU REALIZE THAT?
YOU AND TARA CAN COVER WHILE ED'S AWAY--

THAT'S NOT WHAT I MEAN.
I MEAN IF YOU SEND ED TO IRAQ...

"...THERE'S A VERY GOOD CHANCE WE WON'T EVEN RECOVER HIS BODY."
PUB
London
THE IMPERIAL STAR
PUBLIC HOUSE
ON SALE TODAY!
20% OFF!
THE IMPERIAL STAR
PUBLIC HOUSE
GO!
DRY

FRANCE
ALLEZ
LES BLE
ENGLAND
GO
ENGLAND!
GO
ENGLAND
2002 FIFA WORLD CUP
KOREA JAPAN
GREG RUCKA
LEANDRO FERNANDEZ

CHAPTER 3

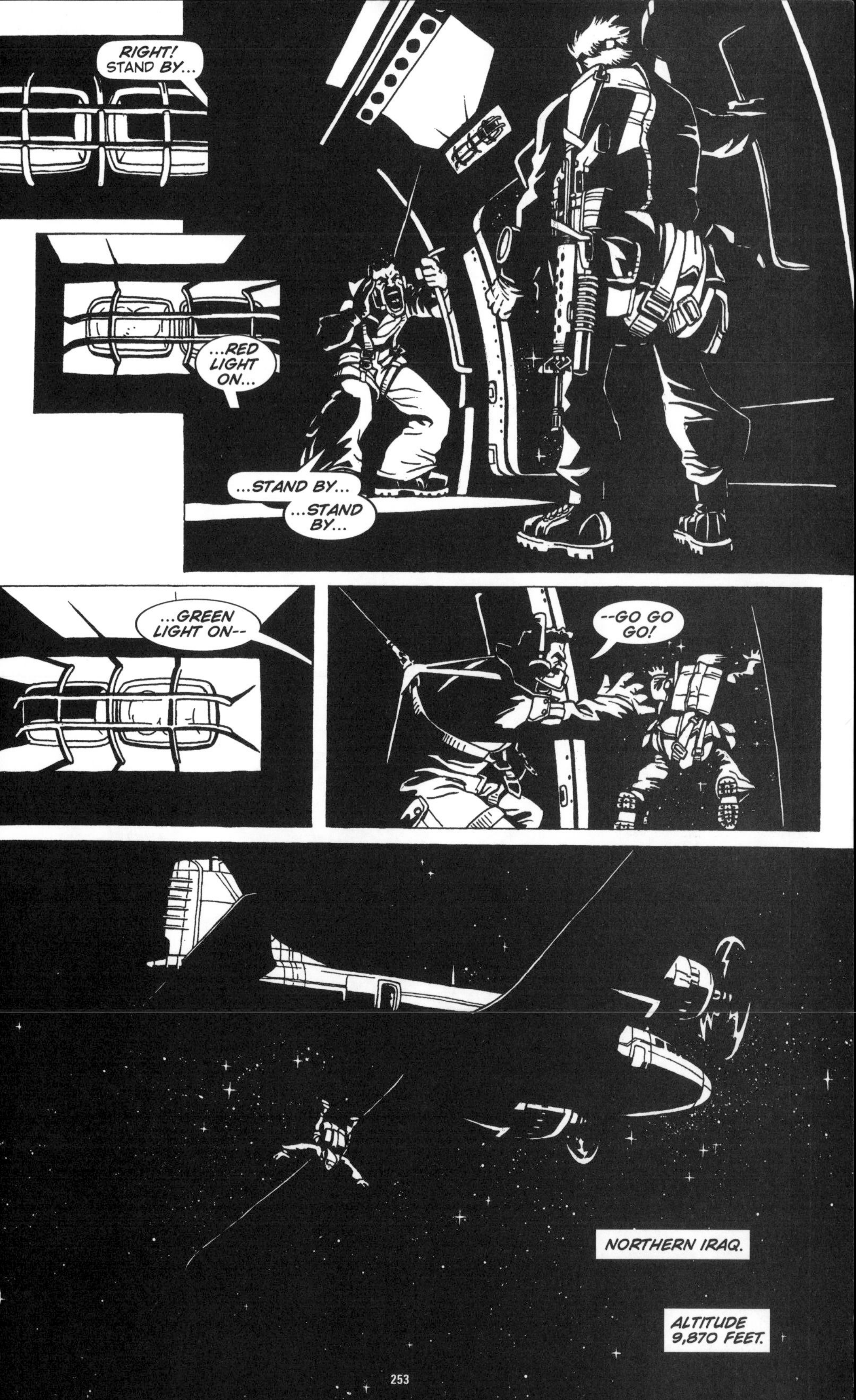

RIGHT! STAND BY...

...RED LIGHT ON...

...STAND BY...

...STAND BY...

"...THOUGHT WE'D HAVE MORE TIME.
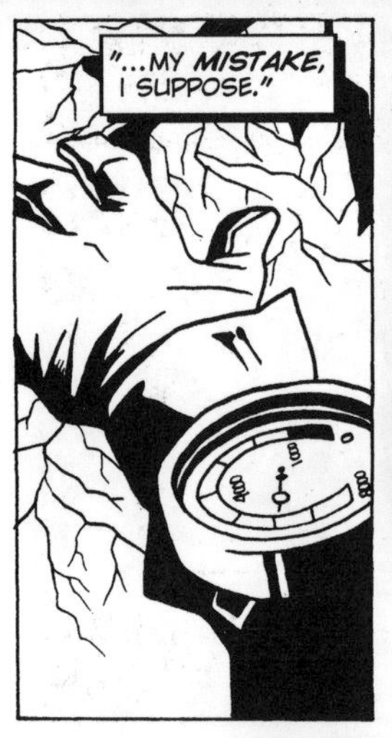
"...MY MISTAKE, I SUPPOSE."

OF COURSE I'M CONCERNED.
NICE WAY OF SHOWING IT.
WHAT DO YOU WANT ME TO SAY, ED?
GOOD LUCK? BE CAREFUL?

THIS.
I WON'T PLAY YOUR FRETTING GIRLFRIEND.
DON'T ASK ME TO.

IT DOESN'T MATTER.
ARE YOU ANGRY AT ME?
DON'T BE DAFT, ED...

"...IT'S NOT AS IF WE DIDN'T KNOW THIS WOULD HAPPEN."

NO... JUST THAT IT CAME UP SO SUDDENLY.
AND IT IS IRAQ...
WHAT DO YOU WANT ME TO SAY?
I DON'T WANT YOU TO SAY ANYTHING. I JUST THOUGHT IT MIGHT CONCERN YOU...

IOSE ARE START."

BUT THAT'S NOT WHAT YOU WANT, IS IT?
I WON'T DO THIS, ED. I WON'T.
DO WHAT?

"DAMMIT, TARA. DO WHAT?"

"I WON'T DO IT..."

...I CAN'T.

LONDON.

SIR? WE'RE *CONFIRMED,* CRYSTAL BALL WENT WHEELS *UP* SEVENTY-THREE MINUTES AGO...

03 JUNE 2002 0037 HOURS GMT

ALN SITHI

BAGDAD

OPERATION: CRYSTAL BALL

STATUS: RUNNING

...MINDER THREE SHOULD BE AT THE *INSERTION* POINT ANY MOMENT NOW.

WELL THAT'S THAT, THEN.
TOO LATE TO ABORT NOW.
CONFIRMATION FROM ANKARA STATION SOONEST. HAVE IT BROUGHT UP BY HAND, I DON'T WANT ANYTHING ON THE INTERNAL LINE.
YES, SIR.
RON? PULL THE MAPS, I WANT TO SEE IT AGAIN.

SHOULD TOUCH DOWN ELEVEN KILOMETERS EAST OF ALN SITHI.
ONCE ON THE GROUND, MINDER THREE DITCHES THE DROP GEAR, THEN SECURES HIS PERIMETER.
IF HE THEN DETERMINES HIS PRESENCE HAS NOT YET BEEN DETECTED, HE MAKES A STRAIGHT PUSH TO THE VILLAGE...

...WITH THE GOAL OF CLOSING ON TARGET BEFORE DAWN.
SUN-UP IN ZONE?
OH-FIVE-FIFTY, LOCAL.
CHRIST...

...THAT GIVES HIM LESS THAN TWO HOURS, ASSUMING HE DIDN'T SNAP HIS LEGS ON LANDING.

HE TAKES AN L.U.P. ON REACHING TARGET?
NO, SIR. WE CONSIDERED A LYING-UP POSITION, BUT THE C.I.A. INTEL MAKES THAT IMPOSSIBLE.
MUGNIYEH IS TO BE MET BY S.S.O. OFFICERS AT MID-DAY, SO THERE'S JUST THE ONE CHANCE TO CATCH HIM IN THE OPEN.

SO NOW IT'S BROAD DAYLIGHT, AND ED'S OPENING FIRE.
MINDER THREE IS AT HIS DISCRETION TO DETERMINE MEANS AND METHOD.

IF HE'S BEEN BLOWN, THEN WHAT?
IF ABLE, HE CONTINUES TO TARGET IN THE HOPES OF COMPLETING THE MISSION. IF THE TARGET IS LOCKED, BUT HE'S STILL AT LIBERTY...

...HE'LL ENTER STANDARD E&E WITH THE HOPE OF MAKING ONE OF THE R.V.S ON THE BORDER WITH TURKEY.
AND IF HE'S NOT AT LIBERTY, HE'S DEAD, SO IT'S NOT REALLY AN ISSUE, IS IT?

RIGHT, THAT'LL DO, RON. THANKS.

MINDER ONE, MY OFFICE.

...SOD YOUR AMBASSADOR, ANGELA.
WE'LL HAVE CONFIRMATION FROM ANKARA THAT HE'S ON THE GROUND WITHIN TWO HOURS...

...WELL THEN THE SOONER THE BETTER...
...NO, AS SOON AS I HEAR, YOU'LL BE INFORMED...

...WELL, YOU CAN TELL HIM THAT YOURSELF, ASSUMING HE MAKES IT OUT ALIVE.

BITCH.
THAT'S NO WAY TO TALK OF OUR MATES IN THE C.I.A..

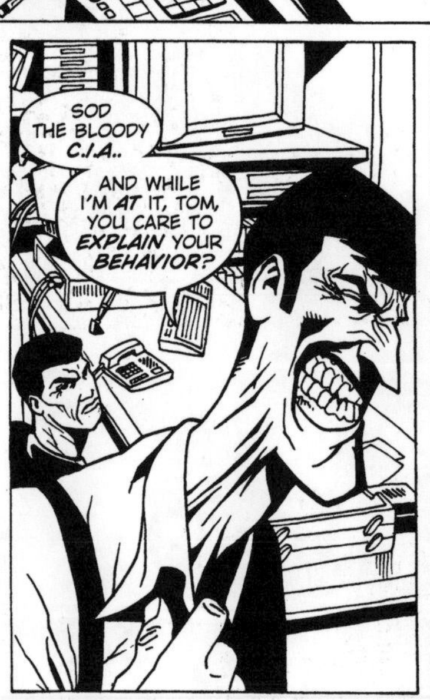
SOD THE BLOODY C.I.A..
AND WHILE I'M AT IT, TOM, YOU CARE TO EXPLAIN YOUR BEHAVIOR?

WHAT BEHAVIOR, EXACTLY, ARE YOU REFERRING TO?
SIR.

I DON'T NEED MY HEAD OF SECTION HAMSTRINGING MORALE IN THE OPS ROOM.
AH, NO, THAT'S MOST CERTAINLY NOT WHAT YOU NEED.

WHAT'S THAT SUPPOSED TO MEAN?
YOU NEED TO MAKE AN APPOINTMENT WITH CALLARD.

ED'S MAYBE LYING IN A WADI IN NORTHERN IRAQ WITH A PAIR OF BROKEN LEGS, IN WHICH CASE HE'S AS GOOD AS DEAD.
IF HE'S NOT-- WHICH WOULD BE A SMALL MIRACLE-- HE'S OFF TO KILL A MAN WE BOTH KNOW ISN'T IMAD MUGNIYEH...
...DESPITE WHAT ANGELA CHENG MAY BE TELLING US.

EVEN IF IT GOES OFF, ED'LL HAVE TO TAB IT TO TURKEY WITH GOD KNOWS HOW MANY MEN LOOKING FOR HIM.
AND FOR WHAT?

SO THE C.I.A. WILL SHARE INTEL THEY ALREADY HAVE, AND THAT WE ONLY MAYBE NEED BECAUSE YOUSSEF HAS US DANCING ON A STRING.
SOUNDS RIGHT. WHERE'S THE PROBLEM?

THE PROBLEM IS THAT IT'S A STUPID REASON FOR ED TO DIE.

WE HAVEN'T EVEN CONFIRMED THAT YOUSSEF IS A MEMBER OF THE G.I.A..

BUT IF HE IS, THEN ED'S JUST BOUGHT US A CHANCE TO PREVENT A MAJOR C.B.W. INCIDENT.
SOUND GOOD AT HIS WAKE, WON'T IT?
IT'S HIS JOB, TOM. YOURS, TOO, LAST I CHECKED.

NOW SHOVE OFF HOME AND GET SOME SLEEP. I'VE GOT WORK TO DO.

THE PIT
OPS ROOM JUST GOT CONFIRMATION FROM ANKARA...
...THEY SAW THE CHUTE OPEN SOMEWHERE AROUND 500 FEET.
SHOULD HAVE BEEN JUST ENOUGH TIME TO ARREST HIS DESCENT.
THANKS.

TOM?
HMM?
YOU DID LA-LO IN THE PARAS?

TRAINING YES. ONLY ONE LIVE JUMP.
BLOODY NIGHTMARE THAT WAS, TOO. LOW-ALTITUDE JUMPS ARE BAD ENOUGH...

...LOW-ALTITUDE LOW-OPENING, FULL KIT, INTO A HOSTILE THEATRE...
...NOT MY IDEA OF FUN.
WHY? THINKING OF TAKING IT UP AS A HOBBY?

HARDLY.
I QUALIFIED STANDARD AND NIGHT, AND THAT WAS MORE THAN ENOUGH DRAMA FOR ME, THANK YOU.

HE'LL BE FINE, YOU KNOW.
I'M SURE.

PAUL?
ANGELA CHENG IS BEING ESCORTED UP FROM *RECEPTION*.

HAVE HER BROUGHT DOWN TO THE OPS ROOM.
GET *D. INT* AND MINDER *TWO* DOWN THERE, AS WELL.
YES, SIR.

OLIVER SAYS THE DEPUTY CHIEF KNOWS THAT KITTERING IS IN NORTHERN IRAQ.

WHAT ELSE?

JUST THAT.
SHALL I TELL HIM YOU'LL BE COMING TO SEE HIM?

IF IT WOULDN'T BE A *BOTHER*, KATE, YES, THANK YOU.

SIMON, THANKS FOR COMING DOWN.
NO TROUBLE.
RON, PUT THESE UP ON OVERLAY...

...THE REST ARE FOR SIMON, THERE, AND WOULD SOMEONE TELL ME WHY THE HELL DAVID ALLEN IS ON THE M.C.O. DESK?
LEX IS THIRTY-SIX OFF, SIR. DAVID'S FILLING IN UNTIL WE CAN SECOND SOMEONE MORE APPROPRIATE.
TOP SECRET U.S. U.K. EYES ONLY
DAVID?
SIR?

I'VE GOT ONE MAJOR OP RUNNING AND ANOTHER IN THE OFFING.
ANY REPEAT OF BANGLADESH AND YOU'RE OUT, UNDERSTOOD?

YES, SIR.
ANGELA?
"CRYSTAL BALL"?

YOU'RE CALLING IT "CRYSTAL BALL"?
IT'S WHAT THE COMPUTER SPAT OUT.
BETTER THAN "INFINITE JUSTICE," CERTAINLY.
THAT WASN'T OUR FAULT...

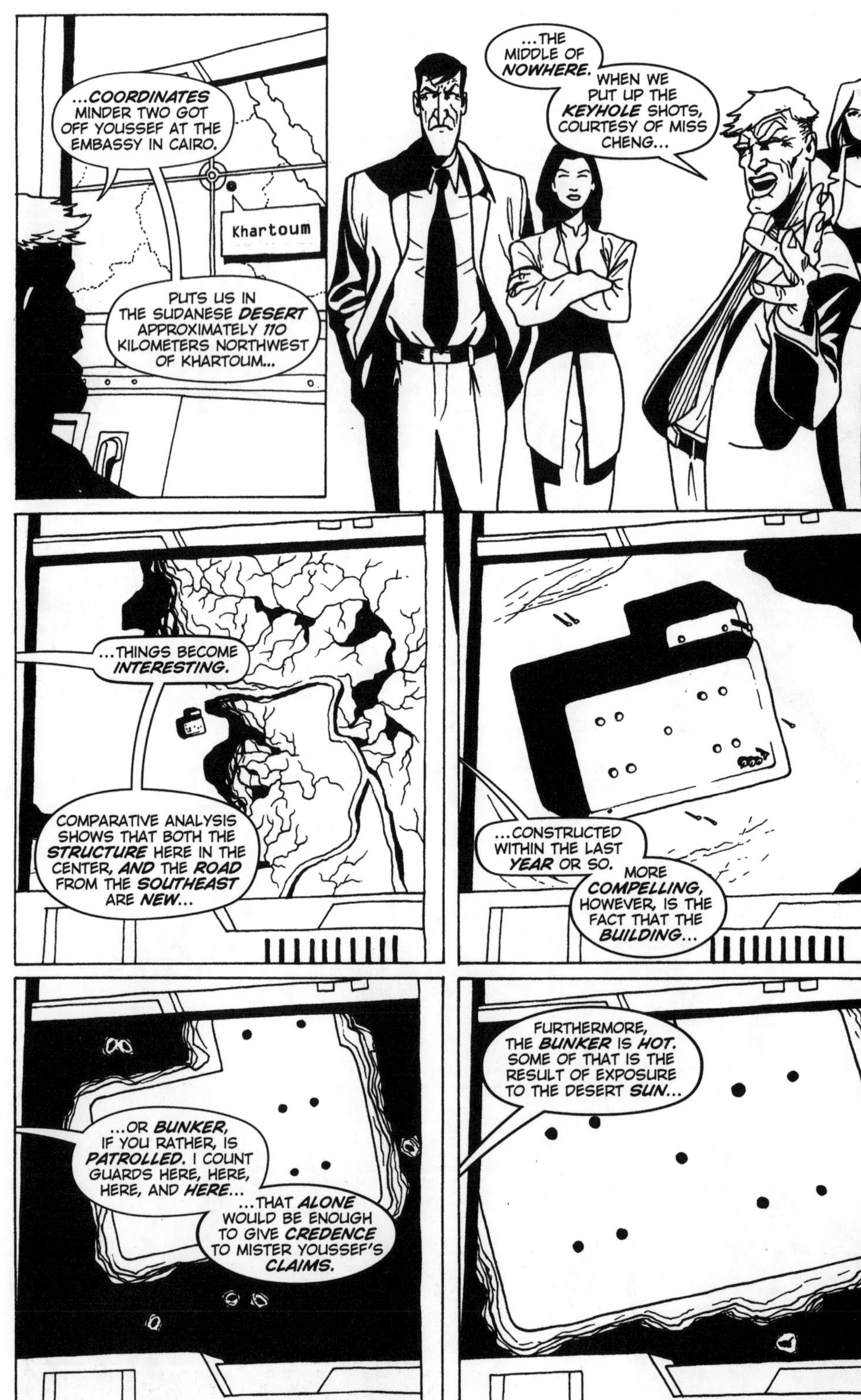
...COORDINATES MINDER TWO GOT OFF YOUSSEF AT THE EMBASSY IN CAIRO.
Khartoum
PUTS US IN THE SUDANESE DESERT APPROXIMATELY 110 KILOMETERS NORTHWEST OF KHARTOUM...
...THE MIDDLE OF NOWHERE.
WHEN WE PUT UP THE KEYHOLE SHOTS, COURTESY OF MISS CHENG...
...THINGS BECOME INTERESTING.
COMPARATIVE ANALYSIS SHOWS THAT BOTH THE STRUCTURE HERE IN THE CENTER, AND THE ROAD FROM THE SOUTHEAST ARE NEW...
...CONSTRUCTED WITHIN THE LAST YEAR OR SO.
MORE COMPELLING, HOWEVER, IS THE FACT THAT THE BUILDING...
...OR BUNKER, IF YOU RATHER, IS PATROLLED. I COUNT GUARDS HERE, HERE, HERE, AND HERE...
...THAT ALONE WOULD BE ENOUGH TO GIVE CREDENCE TO MISTER YOUSSEF'S CLAIMS.
FURTHERMORE, THE BUNKER IS HOT. SOME OF THAT IS THE RESULT OF EXPOSURE TO THE DESERT SUN...

...BUT THERE'S NO DOUBT THAT A LOT OF POWER IS BEING USED INSIDE.

SO YOUSSEF'S ON THE LEVEL?
HIS STORY JUST BECAME INFINITELY MORE PLAUSIBLE, MISS CHACE.

TARA?
RIGHT AWAY, SIR.
AND ANGELA, IF YOU'LL LET ME SEE YOU OUT...?

I DON'T GET TO STAY FOR THE BRIEFING?
YOU'VE DONE MORE THAN ENOUGH ALREADY...

RIGHT, THEN. THERE'S A FLIGHT TO ROME AT TWENTY-TWO TWENTY WE CAN PUT YOU ON....

SIR?
I... UH...
OVER HERE, PAUL.
PAPER JUST SEEMS TO KEEP GROWING, DOESN'T IT?

THAT IT DOES, SIR.
KITTERING'S IN IRAQ, I UNDERSTAND.
YES, SIR.

WITHOUT FOREIGN OFFICE APPROVAL.
YES, SIR.
YOU HAVE ONE MINUTE TO EXPLAIN WHY I SHOULDN'T DEMAND TO 'C' THAT YOU BE FIRED, PAUL.

START TALKING.

THE C.I.A. BELIEVE IMAD MUGNIYEH IS IN THE NORTH OF IRAQ.
FOR THEIR ASSISTANCE IN CONFIRMING THE YOUSSEF STORY, THEY DEMANDED WE SEND A MINDER IN AFTER HIM.

THE C.I.A. WANTED A MINDER TO TAKE MUGNIYEH?
THOSE WERE THEIR TERMS.

HAVE THEY CONFIRMED YOUSSEF'S STORY?
TO THE BEST OF THEIR ABILITY.
YOUSSEF'S NOW CREDIBLE ENOUGH FOR ME TO SEND MINDER TWO TO ROME FOR THE SECOND MEETING.
I SEE.

YOU'LL HAVE TO NOTIFY THE FOREIGN OFFICE AT ONCE ABOUT CRYSTAL BALL.
I'D RATHER WAIT, SIR.

WHY?
WE DON'T KNOW IF KITTERING WILL MAKE IT OUT ALIVE. IF WE NOTIFY NOW, IT BECOMES OFFICIAL.
I'D RATHER GIVE THE FOREIGN OFFICE DENIABILITY IN CASE HE'S CAUGHT, SPIN KITTERING AS A ROGUE.

WHEN'S HE DUE?
TOMORROW, DAWN. WE'LL KNOW BY THEN.
YES...ALL RIGHT, I'LL INFORM 'C.'
THERE'S THE ISSUE OF YOUSSEF'S FIVE HUNDRED THOUSAND POUNDS BEFORE HE MEETS WITH CHACE.

I'LL SEE THAT IT'S AUTHORIZED.
THANK YOU, SIR.

MAKE SURE CHACE GETS OUR MONEY'S WORTH.
OF COURSE, SIR.
AND PAUL...?

DON'T DO IT AGAIN.

OF COURSE NOT, SIR.

ROME.

‹ ...LONG YOU WILL BE STAYING? ›
‹ JUST THROUGH TOMORROW NIGHT. ›

‹ ENJOY YOUR VISIT, MISTER RAHEDI. ›
‹ THANK YOU. ›

‹...AND A BOTTLE OF WINE, PLEASE.›
‹...YES, ROOM EIGHT-OH-THREE, THANK YOU.›

GITANES

NOK
NOK
NOK
‹ROOM SERVICE...›

‹...MAY WE CLEAR YOUR TRAY?›

...YOU ALL *LONELY* THEN?

WHAT?

04 JUNE 2002 1609 HOURS GMT

OPERATION: CRYSTAL BALL

STATUS: RUNNING

ITALY

MEDITERRANEAN SEA

IRAQ

ALL THE *MINDERS* RUNNING ABOUT, YOU'RE STILL *HERE*.

FIGURE YOU'RE FEELING A TAD LEFT *OUT* RIGHT ABOUT NOW.

YOU'VE GOT A LOT OF *LIP* FOR A BLOKE WHO'S BEEN *CITED*, DAVID.

I WASN'T *CITED*, AND IT'S UP FOR *REVIEW*.
I'LL BE BACK IN THE *FIELD* IN A COUPLE OF WEEKS.
AND WE'LL ALL BE *DELIGHTED* FOR YOU.
STILL NO WORD FROM ANKARA?

NOTHING. WHAT'S HIS *WINDOW*?
FIVE HOURS, FORTY-NINE MINUTES.

ANYTHING COMES IN, PASS IT ON *IMMEDIATELY*.
I'LL BE WITH D. OPS.
WHAT ABOUT MINDER TWO?

SHE'S IN *ROME*.
WORST THING SHE'S *DUE* IS *PASTA* POISONING.

BOSS?
HE'S *UPSTAIRS,* TOM...

...'C'S BEEN SUMMONED TO DOWNING STREET.
PAUL AND THE DEPUTY CHIEF ARE *BRIEFING* HIM BEFORE HE *GOES.*
THERE A *FLAP?*
NOT *SURE*...

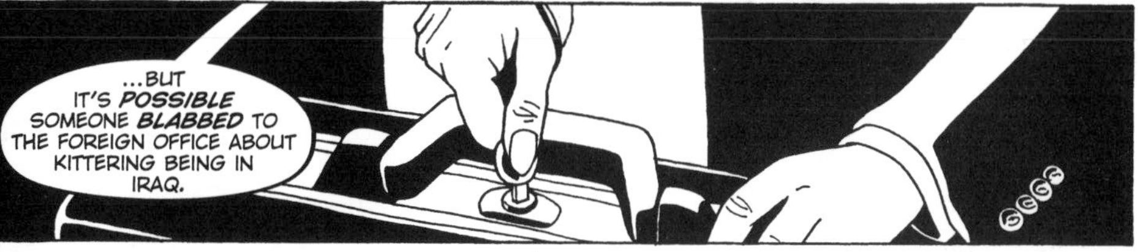
...BUT IT'S *POSSIBLE* SOMEONE *BLABBED* TO THE FOREIGN OFFICE ABOUT KITTERING BEING IN IRAQ.

OH, FOR CHRIST'S SAKE. WELDON JUST COULDN'T KEEP HIS *MOUTH* SHUT, COULD HE?
I SAID IT'S *POSSIBLE.* IT MIGHT BE SOMETHING *ELSE* ENTIRELY.

YOU WANT TO *WAIT?*
NOT MUCH ELSE TO DO RIGHT NOW.

AT LEAST, NOT FOR ANOTHER *FIVE* AND A *HALF* HOURS OR SO....

...BE CONNECTED TO MISTER RAHEDI'S ROOM.

...CAN YOU CHECK *AGAIN*, PLEASE?
...WHEN?... I SEE...NO, THANK YOU....

"M.C.O., GO."
"CHACE, ZED DELTA INDIGO EIGHT THREE THREE, REQUEST *SECURE.*"

"WE ARE SECURE, GO AHEAD."
"THAT YOU, DAVID? I NEED EITHER TOM OR D. OPS, WHOMEVER IS NEARER."

"WALLACE IS RIGHT HERE, HOLD ON."

"TARA? WHAT'S HAPPENED?"
"NOT SURE...

"...BUT I THINK YOUSSEF'S BEEN *BLOWN*...

"...THE HOTEL SAID HE'D *CHECKED* OUT, AND WHEN I LEFT THE PLACE I GRABBED A *TAIL.*"

"YOU BACKED IT?"
"WASN'T THAT *HARD* TO DO."

"WHAT'D YOU GET?"

"TWO OF THEM, A MAN AND A WOMAN...
35

"...I FOLLOWED THEM BACK TO AN APARTMENT. THEY'RE INSIDE NOW, SO I THOUGHT I'D TAKE THE CHANCE TO CALL IN."

"WHAT ARE YOU GOING TO DO?"
"FIGURED I'D TAKE A LOOK INSIDE IF THE OPPORTUNITY PRESENTED ITSELF."

"RIGHT...BE CAREFUL, TARA. COULD BE THEY WANTED YOU TO MAKE THE TAIL."
"I WILL. TOM?"

"HMM?"
"ANY WORD ON CRYSTAL BALL?"

"HE'S GOT UNTIL DAWN, TARA."
"I WAS ONLY--"
TASSI DELLE PERIFERIE
0800 444 3987

"I DON'T CARE. YOU KEEP YOUR HEAD IN ROME, TARA.

"CALL IN WHEN YOU GET CLEA

HELLO?
IS ANYONE HOME?
CORRIERE

CUKURCA, TURKEY.
72 KM NNE OF ALN SITHI, IRAQ.
HI, I'M ED.
YOU WOULDN'T HAVE ANYTHING TO DRINK, WOULD YOU?

CHAPTER 4

SUDAN.
HELIUM

HELIUM

ROME.
CAVALIERI HILTON
TARA? D. OPS.
YOUSSEF'S DEAD.
BLOODY HELL. WHAT HAPPENED?
I'M NOT CERTAIN.
I FOUND HIM IN THE BATHROOM OF THE FLAT.
HE'D BEEN TORTURED.
DID YOU GET A LOOK AROUND?
BRIEFLY. WASN'T THE TIME TO LOITER.
THERE WAS NOTHING THERE. I THINK THE G.I.A. WERE USING IT AS A SAFE HOUSE.
THE ONES WHO WERE TAILING YOU?
THEY KILLED HIM, I'M SURE OF IT. I SAW THEM LEAVE BEFORE I WENT INSIDE.
THEY'RE BACK IN PARIS BY NOW.

I WANT YOU ON THE NEXT FLIGHT HOME.
YES, SIR.
SIR? WHAT'S THE STATUS ON CRYSTAL BALL?

SIR...?

...FROM MINDER TWO, IN ROME. SHE'S ON HER WAY HOME NOW.

YOUSSEF BLEW HIS RENDEZVOUS AT THE BARBERINI. WHEN CHACE LEFT THE HOTEL, SHE'D PICKED UP A TAIL.
G.I.A.?
THAT'S HER ASSESSMENT. SHE BROKE THE TAIL, THEN BACKED IT TO A SAFE HOUSE IN TRASTEVERE. WAITED OUTSIDE ALL NIGHT.

THIS MORNING THE TWO WHO'D TAILED HER SHOVED OFF AND SHE GOT A LOOK AROUND INSIDE.
SHE FOUND YOUSSEF, DEAD. HE'D BEEN TORTURED.
ANY IDEA HOW MUCH HE TALKED BEFORE HE DIED?

DEPENDS ON WHEN THEY KILLED HIM, BUT AT A GUESS, EVERYTHING.
SO WE'VE JUST GIVEN THE G.I.A. FIVE HUNDRED THOUSAND POUNDS?

WE'LL HAVE A HARD TIME DEFENDING THE LOSS OF THE MONEY, SIR.
THAT'S HARDLY RELEVANT!
BUDGET IS ALWAYS RELEVANT! ASIDE FROM THE FACT THAT WE MAY HAVE JUST FUNDED THE G.I.A. FOR THE NEXT FIVE YEARS!

THAT MONEY CAME OUT OF YOUR OPERATIONAL FUND.
ENOUGH.
WHERE DOES THIS LEAVE US WITH REGARD TO YOUSSEF'S INFORMATION?

RIGHT WHERE WE STARTED, I'M AFRAID.
WE STILL HAVE THE KEYHOLE DATA. THE COORDINATES SHOWED A FACILITY IN THE SUDAN.
D. INT BELIEVES THAT'S WHERE THEY'RE MANUFACTURING THE SARIN.
DO WE HAVE ANY EVIDENCE OF THAT?
NOTHING CONCLUSIVE. THE FACILITY COULD BE USED TO MAKE ANYTHING.
THEY'RE NOT GOING TO PUT A SIGN UP SAYING "NERVE GAS MADE HERE," ARE THEY?
NO, THEY'D HARDLY BE SO HELPFUL.
WHICH BRINGS US TO THE QUESTION. WHAT DO YOU WANT TO DO NEXT?
I WANT S.A.S. INTO SUDAN. FULL ASSAULT ON THE FACILITY, RECOVERY OF ANY DATA OR INFORMATION INSIDE.
YOU'RE MAD.
IN THE NEXT THREE WEEKS A SARIN GAS ATTACK WILL BE LAUNCHED AGAINST U.K. CITIZENS.
WE'RE RUNNING OUT OF TIME AND WE'VE RUN OUT OF LEADS.
YOU'LL NEVER GET M.O.D. APPROVAL TO PUT S.A.S. INTO SUDAN, PAUL!
SIR, IF YOU CONVINCED THE PRIME MINISTER--
THERE'S NO REASON TO BELIEVE SUCH AN ASSAULT WOULD--
GENTLEMEN.

CAN'T BE DONE, PAUL.
SIR...
IT CAN'T BE DONE, PAUL...
...NOT WITHOUT CONCRETE PROOF, AND NOT SO SOON AFTER PUTTING KITTERING INTO IRAQ.
THE ONE HAS NO BEARING ON THE OTHER.
THE PRIME MINISTER WOULD DISAGREE.
BAD ENOUGH YOU SENT MINDER THREE INTO IRAQ WITHOUT FOREIGN OFFICE APPROVAL.
THE P.M. WILL NOT COUNTENANCE A SECOND S.I.S. INITIATED ARMED INCURSION AGAINST A SOVEREIGN GOVERNMENT SO SOON AFTER THE FIRST.
IT ALREADY LOOKS LIKE WE'RE TRYING TO START A WAR, PAUL.
NO, JUST TRYING TO FIGHT IT.
IF YOUSSEF WASN'T ON THE LEVEL, WHY DID THE G.I.A. HAVE HIM KILLED?
HE MUST HAVE BEEN TELLING CHACE THE TRUTH.
A COMPELLING ARGUMENT. BUT ONE THAT WON'T PUT THE S.A.S. INTO SUDAN.
YOUSSEF WAS OUR PROOF.
WITHOUT HIM, WE'RE IN THE DARK.

FIND *SOMETHING*, PAUL.
I'LL HAPPILY GO TO DOWNING STREET AND *FIGHT* FOR YOU...

...BUT I'LL NEED *AMMUNITION*.
BRING IT TO ME, I'LL GET YOU THE S.A.S.

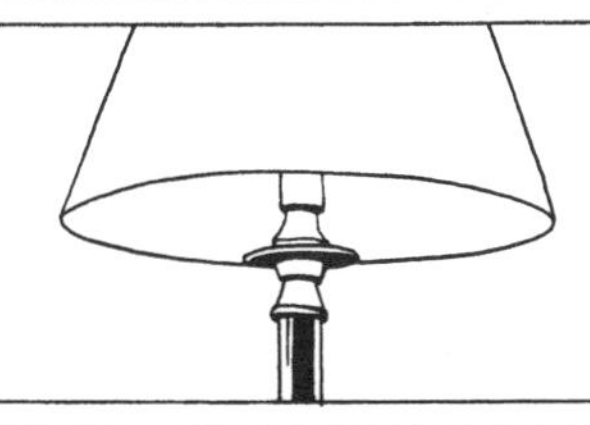

THANK YOU, SIR.

...AND HAIL THE CONQUERING HERO.
BACK FROM IRAQ WITH NOT A SCRATCH TO SHOW FOR IT.
THE PIT
OH, I'VE GOT SCRATCHES...

...JUST NONE THAT I'M WILLING TO SHOW YOU.

WHERE'S MINDER TWO?
OOOH, MINDER TWO, IS IT?
NOT TARA? NOT THE LOVELY MISS CHACE?

YOU MAKE ME SORRY I ASKED.
THE PIT
ON HER WAY BACK FROM ROME.
YOUSSEF DIDN'T PLAY.

HE GOT MADE FOR A LIAR?
HE GOT MADE FOR DEAD.
6
JUNE
2002

TARA'S FINE.

WHEN'S SHE DUE?
BY EVENING.
ED?
HMM?
IT'S GOT TO STOP.
WHAT DOES?
WHATEVER IT IS YOU AND SHE HAVE GOING, IT'S GOT TO STOP.
GET STUFFED.

CAIRO.
Lufthansa
TAXI

Lufthansa
Check in

thansa
Check in
Lufthansa

EGYPT TODAY

nsa
1112
78 MUC
5328 SJJ-
Butmir

CAIRO Times
EGYPT TODAY

LONDON.
TAXI
LONDON
Mrs. Tara Chace
ss Tara Chace
OCCUPANT
Nok Nok

WONDERED WHO IT WAS *WATCHING* ME.
THOUGHT *FIVE* WAS UP TO ONE OF THEIR *RANDOM* CHECKS.

NO, JUST ME.

FORGET IT.

IT'S NOT *WORTH* IT.

10 JUNE
2002
0834 HOURS
GMT
RON?
YES, LOVE?
YOU KNOW THE CAIRO *NUMBER TWO?*

ALEXIS?
IS D. OPS IN?

DEEP IN *MEDITATION.*
LEX? WHAT THE *HELL* ARE YOU DOING OUT OF THE OPS ROOM?
I'M *COVERED,* SIR.

THIS CAME IN THE ROUTINES, FROM THE CAIRO NUMBER TWO. RON THOUGHT YOU SHOULD SEE IT RIGHT *AWAY.*
RON HAVE AN OPINION ON HOW I DEPLOY THE MINDERS, AS WELL?

I'M *SORRY,* SIR?
NEVER *MIND.*
...THIS WAS IN THE *ROUTINES?*
YES, SIR.

RETURN SIGNAL TO CAIRO, *FLASH* PRECEDENCE.
REQUEST *WHOLE* ITINERARY, THEN FIND OUT WHY THE *HELL* IT TOOK WALKER *FOUR* DAYS TO *NOTIFY* US!
RIGHT *AWAY,* SIR.

SIR? CAN YOU MEET ME IN C'S OFFICE RIGHT AWAY?

OVER HERE, GENTLEMEN. HAVING MY MORNING TEA AND INTELLIGENCE.
DAVID WALKER SAYS HE SAW RASHED EL HAGE IN CAIRO THURSDAY EVENING.

WALKER BRIBED THE LUFTHANSA CLERK, GOT HIS FULL ITINERARY. AS OF FRIDAY, HAGE WAS IN SARAJEVO.
REFRESH MY MEMORY, PAUL. WHY IS THIS IMPORTANT?
HAGE IS SAUDI, SIR, WAS PURSUING AN ADVANCED DEGREE IN CHEMISTRY AT CAMBRIDGE TWO YEARS AGO...

...FIVE HAD HIM DEPORTED AFTER THEY DETERMINED HE WAS SUPPLYING MATÉRIEL AND INFORMATION TO E.I.J..
THEY HAD PROOF?
COMPELLING ENOUGH TO EXPEDITE HIS DEPORTATION.

IF THE SUDAN FACILITY IS EQUIPPED TO MAKE SARIN, RASHED EL HAGE IS THE MAN TO RUN IT.
SAUDI INTELLIGENCE HAS BEEN TRYING TO LOCATE HIM SINCE THE SEPTEMBER ELEVEN ATTACKS. HE'D DISAPPEARED.

IT'S ALL CIRCUMSTANTIAL, PAUL.
STILL NOT ENOUGH TO GET S.A.S. INTO SUDAN.

AND IF HAGE WAS IN SUDAN, HE'S MOST LIKELY FINISHED WHATEVER IT WAS HE WAS DOING.
I RECOGNIZE THAT.

THEN WHAT ARE YOU *AFTER?*
PERMISSION TO SEND WALLACE TO SARAJEVO, SEE IF HE CAN PICK UP THE *TRAIL.*
PERMISSION TO RETURN CHACE TO CAIRO, SEE IF SHE CAN LEARN WHY YOUSSEF WAS THERE IN THE *FIRST* PLACE.
TO WHAT *END?*

THE *SAME* END, SIR.
IF IT WAS *HAGE* MAKING THE SARIN, HE MOST LIKELY KNOWS THE *DELIVERY* METHOD *AND* THE *TARGET.*

THE *INTELLIGENCE* IS *FOUR* DAYS *OLD.* BY THE TIME *WALLACE* REACHES SARAJEVO, IT'LL BE *FIVE.*
IT'S BEEN ALMOST A *MONTH* SINCE CHACE WAS IN *CAIRO.*
SEEMS LIKE A *LONGSHOT,* PAUL.

IT *IS,* SIR.
WE'LL *LEAK* WORD OF THEIR RESPECTIVE *ARRIVALS,* AND I'LL *ARM* THEM BOTH ONCE ON *STATION.*

I DON'T *LIKE* IT.

NOR DO *ANY* OF US.
BUT WE'RE *RUNNING* OUT OF *MOVES.*

I'LL SPEAK TO THE FOREIGN OFFICE, LET THEM *KNOW.*

THOUGHT YOU'D BE HEADED STRAIGHT TO THE OPS ROOM.
WALLACE IS WAITING FOR ME.
I WANTED TO SPEAK TO YOU ABOUT THE DELAY IN THE SIGNAL.

I'LL MAKE INQUIRIES.
YOU KNOW WHAT YOU'LL FIND.
COLIN HODGSON IS A PROFESSIONAL, PAUL.
I DON'T SEE HIM DELAYING WALKER'S SIGNAL OUT OF PETTINESS FOR WHATEVER SLIGHT CHACE COMMITTED.

PERCEIVED SLIGHT, SIR. CHACE MAINTAINS THAT HODGSON OVER-REACTED TO HER PRESENCE.
HARDLY SURPRISING, REALLY.

I BEG YOUR PARDON.
HARDLY SURPRISING THAT CHACE MADE HODGSON NERVOUS, PAUL.

AFTER ALL, YOU ARE SENDING THE MINDERS OUT TO BE SHOT AT.
KEEP ME POSTED.

... THE MUSLIM POPULATION HAS SEEN A LARGE DEGREE OF PENETRATION BY ISLAMIC MILITANTS.
SO I CAN EXPECT A FRIENDLY GREETING?
RIGHT, WHERE ARE WE?

COMPLETING MINDER ONE'S BRIEFING NOW, SIR.
OPERATIONS DESIGNATED LONGBOW AND TEA-TREE.
FLIGHTS ARE SET, BOTH MINDERS SHOULD BE IN THEIR THEATRES BEFORE DARK.

GOOD.

WE'RE DROPPING WORD OF BOTH YOUR ARRIVALS.
EACH OF YOU IS TO DRAW ARMS ON STATION.

DO WE HAVE A CHOICE?

NO.

SARAJEVO.

...MISTER WALLACE?

WHO IS IT?

SANYA MILOSKA. YOU'RE EXPECTING ME?

IT'S OPEN.

NONE OF MY INFORMANTS HAVE SEEN HAGE.
OR IF THEY HAVE, THEY'RE NOT TELLING.
WHERE WOULD HE GO?

THERE ARE A FEW PLACES, CAFES AND THE LIKE, THAT THE MILITANTS ARE RUMORED TO FREQUENT.
INFORMATION HAS BEEN DIFFICULT TO GET SINCE THE END OF THE WAR.

I CAN GIVE YOU A LIST OF NAMES AND ADDRESSES.
THAT'D BE VERY HELPFUL, THANK YOU.

WILL YOU USE IT?
THIS THING, YOU MEAN?
YES.

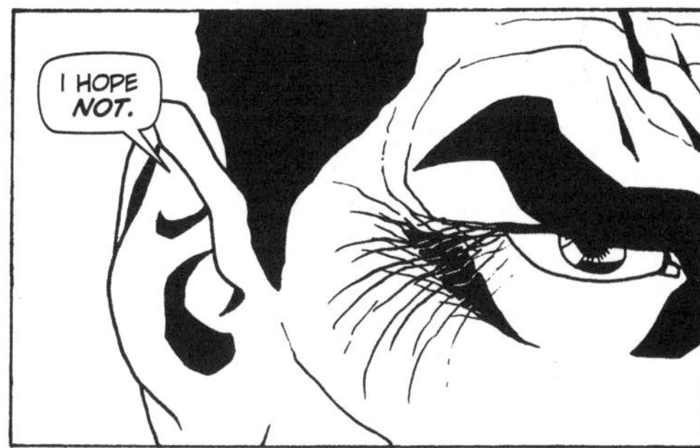
I HOPE NOT.

CAIRO.

CHACE! CHACE!

DAVID WALKER, GET IN.

DROP WORD OF MY ARRIVAL DOESN'T MEAN SHOUT MY NAME IN FRONT OF THE AIRPORT, MISTER WALKER.

AND YOU HAVE MY APOLOGIES...

...BUT I THINK YOU'VE ALREADY WON YOURSELF SOME NEW ADMIRERS.

THEY DON'T WASTE TIME.
YOUSSEF'S A HOT TOPIC RIGHT NOW.
HELP YOURSELF TO THE BRIEFCASE...

...FILE SAYS YOU'RE A P99 GIRL.

NO, I'M MORE THE STAY AT HOME, FANCY A CUPPA GIRL.
WHERE ARE WE HEADED?

YOUR CHOICE. EMBASSY OR HOTEL?
HOTEL WOULD BE BEST.
I CAN GET YOU IN AT THE HILTON.

LOVELY. I COULD USE A HOT BATH.

DON'T SUPPOSE YOU'D WANT COMPANY?
SURE. YOU DON'T KNOW SEAN BEAN, DO YOU?

I CAN MAKE SOME CALLS.
DON'T BOTHER...

...I DOUBT I'LL HAVE THE TIME....

JAPAN.
HANJIN

FRAGILE

HÉLIUM
GREG RUCKA
LEANDRO FERNANDEZ '02

CHAPTER 5

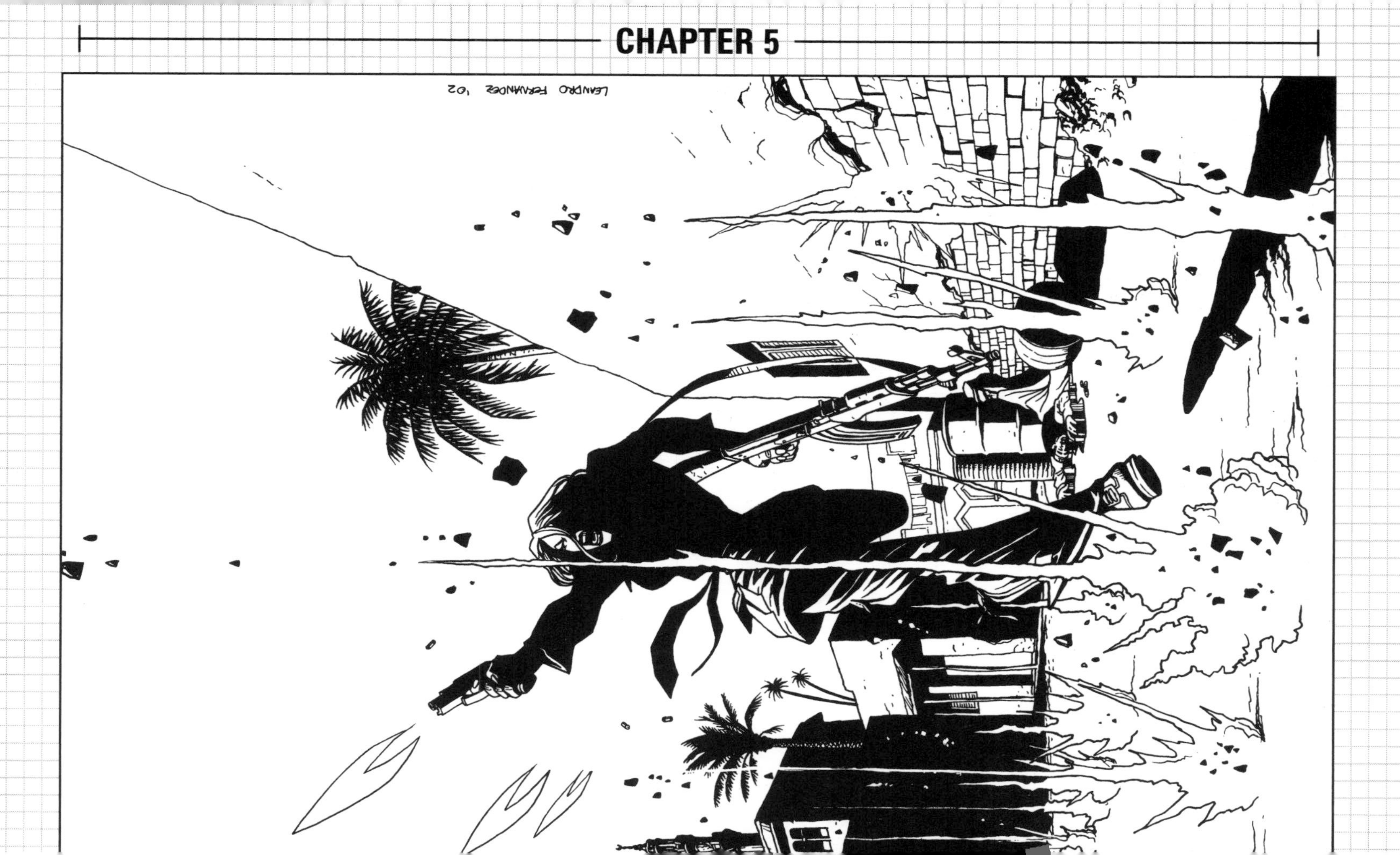

NAGAI STADIUM, OSAKA, JAPAN.

STOP!

<PURPOSE OF VISIT?>
<STOCKING FOR THE WEDNESDAY MATCH. NATIONAL BALLOONS, FLAGS, HELIUM, LIKE THAT.>

<ALL RIGHT, HAVE YOUR CREW COME OVER HERE, PLEASE.>

<TRUST ME, I KNOW...>
<THIS GETS OLD FAST.>

<...AND WE'RE STILL IN THE FIRST ROUND.>
HELIUM
HELIUM

<WAIT UNTIL THE QUARTER-FINALS...>

<...WE'LL BE DOING CAVITY SEARCHES.>
<GOD, I HOPE YOU'RE JOKING-->
<SIR? EXCUSE ME...>

<...HOW MANY CANISTERS ARE LISTED IN THE MANIFEST?>

<LET ME CHECK.>
<PROBLEM?>

<WAIT HERE.>

<YOU'RE A CANISTER *SHORT*.>
<IT HAD A *LEAK*. I CALLED KOBE, THEY'RE SENDING A *REPLACEMENT* FROM THE WAREHOUSE.>

<HERE YOU *GO*.>
<JUST FOLLOW THE *RAMP* TO THE END, YOU CAN *UNLOAD* THERE.>
<THANKS.>

SARAJEVO.

NORMALLY I'D SAY LET *ME* DO THE *TALKING*, SANYA...

THAT WOULD REQUIRE YOU KNOWING THE *LANGUAGE*, TOM.

MY POINT *EXACTLY*.

JUST MAKE IT *CLEAR* THAT YOU'RE TRANSLATING FOR *ME*, EVEN IF YOU *AREN'T*.

WHY?

I WANT THEM *ANGRY* WITH ME, *NOT* YOU.

EXCUSE ME!

CAN YOU HELP ME?
<THE HELL IS YOUR PROBLEM? I'M WATCHING THE GAME.>

SORRY TO INTERRUPT, VE JUST A *QUICK* QUESTION...
<HE APOLOGIZES FOR BEING SO *RUDE,* AND WISHES ONLY TO ASK A *BRIEF* QUESTION OF YOU...>

...I'M LOOKING FOR A *FRIEND,* I'M WONDERING IF YOU'VE *SEEN* HIM...
<...HE IS *SEARCHING* FOR HIS *FRIEND,* BUT CANNOT FIND HIM *ANYWHERE...*>

<...HE WONDERS IF YOU HAVE *SEEN* HIM?>

<NO, I HAVE *NOT.* THE *ARABS* DON'T COME IN *HERE* ANYMORE. TRY DOWN THE *STREET.*>

HE SAYS TO TRY FURTHER DOWN THE BLOCK.
SEEMED A TAD *HOSTILE,* DIDN'T HE?
WHAT DID YOU *EXPECT,* TOM...

2002
FIFA WORLD CUP
KOREA JAPAN
2002 5.31 - 6.30
...YOU *INTERRUPTED* THE *MATCH.*

37 KM EAST OF CAIRO, ROUTE 33.
...SAME ONE AS YESTERDAY.
AS-SUWAIS 40 k

MIGHT I ASK WHAT YOU DID LAST NIGHT?
ASSUMING THE E.I.J. MOVED THE SARIN THROUGH EGYPT ON ROUTE TO TARGET, IT HAD TO BE SHIPPED SOMEHOW.
THAT'S WHAT I TRIED TO LEARN LAST NIGHT, AND THAT'S WHY WE'RE HEADING TO SUEZ NOW...
...AND MAYBE THAT'S WHY SOMEONE DOESN'T WANT US GETTING THERE.
THEY'RE CLOSING UP.
PROBABLY GOING TO TRY TO FORCE US OFF THE MAIN ROAD, INTO AN AMBUSH.
LET THEM.

RELAX, DAVID. I'VE DONE THIS BEFORE.
THAT'S WONDERFUL, TARA. I HAVEN'T.

FOLLOW VEHICLE IS THE PLUG. WHEN YOU SEE THE STOPPER, HIT THE BRAKES AND THEN GET INTO COVER FAST.
I'LL DO THE REST.
HERE WE GO.

WE'RE ON.

IF WE WERE EXPECTING TO FIND HIM, YES...
I THINK THE WORD IS GOOSE-CHASE?

...BUT SINCE ALL I WANT IS SOME ATTENTION, I'D SAY IT'S WORKING BEAUTIFULLY.
THERE ARE EASIER WAYS TO GET ATTENTION, TOM.

NOT WHAT I HAD IN MIND....

YOU SAW HIM?
PICKED US UP AT THE OTHER CAFÉ, I THINK...

...I DON'T RECOGNIZE...
...TOM?
SORRY.

HMMM

HHHOO

OOOUUNN

IT'S A KINK, I KNOW...

...BUT I FIND IT'S THE ONLY WAY I CAN GET PEOPLE TALKING.
<NO! PLEASE MY MISTAKE, I THOUGHT YOU WERE LOOKING TO BUY THE TICKETS-->

<--THE SAUDI'S TICKETS I KNOW WHO HAS THEM...>
TOM...

...HE'S TALKING ABOUT A SAUDI....

GO
GET COVER
GO!

TOLD YOU TO GET TO COVER.
AND HAVE CROCKER TEAR ME A NEW ONE WHEN YOU ENDED UP DEAD? NOT ON YOUR LIFE.
I COUNT THREE MORE.
MOVING TO FLANK, PROBABLY.

PUTTING A LOT OF EFFORT INTO THIS, DON'T YOU THINK?
YES.
MAKES YOU WONDER WHY, DOESN'T IT?
GOING FOR THE LONG GUN.
COVER ME.
GOT IT.
DEFINITELY THREE.
RELOADING.

HOW FAST ARE YOU?
WHEN SOMEONE'S SHOOTING AT ME?
I'M BLOODY CARL LEWIS.

HOLD THIS.
YOU LYING?

DOES IT MATTER?
YOU'RE THE BETTER SHOT, TARA

MAKE FOR THE FIRST HOUSE WE PASSED ON THE WAY IN.

DON'T STOP, NO MATTER WHAT YOU HEAR.

DAVID? YOU ALL RIGHT?
THINK SO, YES...
...I'LL TAKE A LOOK AT THEIR CAR.

TARA? YOU MIGHT WANT TO TAKE A LOOK AT THIS...

WHAT'VE YOU GOT?
NOT SURE. BUT I DON'T THINK THESE BLOKES WERE WORKING IN SUEZ...

...AT LEAST ONE OF THEM WAS WORKING FOR AN AIR FREIGHT COMPANY OUT OF CAIRO.
NAME?

QUADRAT TRANSPORTATION.
WHY DO I KNOW THAT NAME?

DROP ME BACK TO THE HOTEL, THEN GET TO THE EMBASSY AND FLASH-PRECEDENCE A SIGNAL TO LONDON. GIVE THEM THE WHOLE THING
UH... SURE...

...WHY?
QUADRAT TRANSPORTATION IS A DIVISION OF QUADRAT CONSTRUCTION.
QUADRAT CONSTRUCTION IS ONE OF THE FRONTS AL-QAE'DA USES IN SUDAN.

SO NOW WE KNOW HOW THEY'RE MOVING IT...
...THE ONLY QUESTION IS WHERE.

<THAT'S HIM, I THOUGHT YOU WERE *WITH* HIM, MAYBE.>
<HOW DO YOU *KNOW* HIM?>
<YOU'RE *NOT* POLICE?>
<NO, YOU HAVE OUR *WORD*.>

<BUT YOU WANT TO *BUY* THE *TICKETS*?>
<TELL ME ABOUT THE *SAUDI*, FIRST.>

<LIKE IN THE *PICTURE*, I *SAID*. HE WAS AT THIS PLACE I GO, HE WAS TALKING ABOUT HAVING THE TICKETS...>
<...YOU *SURE* YOU'RE NOT *COPS*?>
<WE ARE *NOT* COPS.>

<...OKAY... WELL... SOME *FRIENDS* OF *MINE*, THEY *TOOK* HIS *TICKETS*, OKAY?>
<THANKS.>
Shield

<FIGURE THEY'RE *WORTH* A LOT. WORTH *MORE* THAN *DRUGS* MAYBE.>
<YOU *WANT* THEM? OR YOUR *FRIEND*?>

WHAT'S HE SAYING?
IT'S CONFUSING. I THINK HE ROBBED HIM...

...AND NOW HE WANTS TO SELL US THE TICKETS HE TOOK OFF OF EL HAGE.
WHAT, YOU MEAN PLANE TICKETS?

<TELL ME ABOUT THE TICKETS.>

<EXCELLENT TICKETS! THE REAL THING, I'VE SEEN THEM. MIDFIELD SEATS, NAGAI STADIUM, NIGERIA VERSUS ENGLAND...>

THEY'RE CUP TICKETS. ENGLAND VERSUS NIGERIA.
THAT'S TOMORROW'S GAME.

FUCK ME.
I'VE GOT TO CALL LONDON
<WHA--WAIT! WHERE ARE YOU GOING?>

<I DIDN'T EVEN GIVE YOU A PRICE!>

NAGAI STADIUM, OSAKA.
2002
FIFA WORLD CUP
KOREA JAPAN
NIGERIA
NIGERI
PHOTO
20

ENGLAND

6

BECKHAM
7

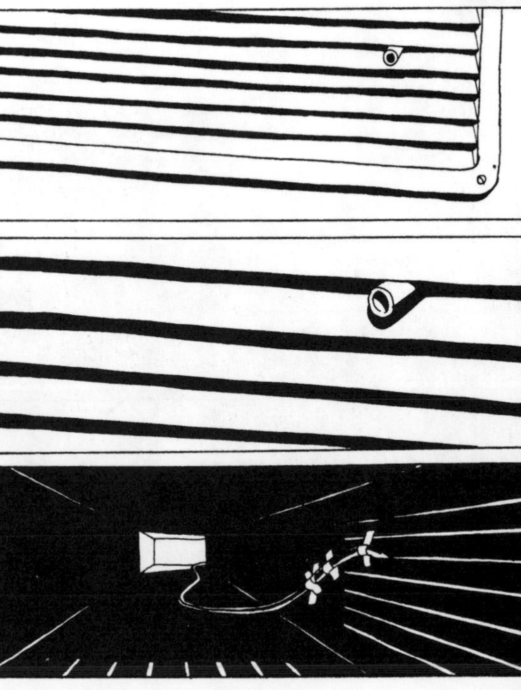

<...TAPED IT DOWN?>
<EXACTLY AS PLANNED...>

<...I EVEN CHECKED FROM INSIDE THE LOCKER ROOM. THERE'S NO WAY TO SPOT THE HOSE.>
<GOOD.>

<KICK-OFF IS AT EIGHT, SO THEY WON'T BE IN THE ROOM UNTIL FIVE, AT LEAST.>
<TIME FOR YOU BOTH TO GET OUT OF THE COUNTRY.>

<DO WE KNOW WHAT HAPPENED TO HAGE? WHY HE DIDN'T COME?>
<NO, AND IT DOES NOT MATTER NOW.>
<IT IS ON ME TO DO THE REST.>
<GOD IS GREAT.>

<GOD IS-->

<NOBODY MOVE NOBODY MOVES!>

<STOP! STOP!>

HELIUM
HELIUM
<CONTROL, ZEBRA ONE. TWO *CAGED*, ONE *CLIPPED*, AND WE HAVE THE *BOX*.>

<REQUEST *HAZMAT* AND *BOMB* TEAMS, VENTILATOR *SIX*.>
<CONFIRMED AND EN ROUTE.>

...JUST RECEIVED FROM THE TOKYO STATION CHIEF...
...JAPANESE SPECIAL FORCES HAVE **LOCATED** AND **REMOVED** FOUR CANISTERS OF **SARIN** FROM NAGAI STADIUM.
THEY WERE PLANNING ON **PIPING** IT INTO THE ENGLISH LOCKER ROOM.
DEAR **LORD**, DID YOU SAY **FOUR** CANISTERS, PAUL?

YES, SIR. MORE THAN ENOUGH TO KILL THE TEAM, ALONG WITH ANYONE ELSE IN THE TUNNELS AT THE TIME.
THEY WERE PROBABLY HOPING IT WOULD RECIRCULATE --ALBEIT WITH LESS POTENCY-- THROUGHOUT THE REST OF THE STADIUM.

THEY SMUGGLED IT IN WITH THE HELIUM FOR THE BALLOON CONCESSIONS.
AND RASHED EL HAGE?
HE'S GONE. WE'LL KEEP SARAJEVO WATCHING FOR HIM...

...BUT I SUSPECT HE'S BACK IN SAUDI ARABIA.
AND WHAT ABOUT WALLACE AND CHACE?

CHACE LANDS AT HEATHROW WITHIN THE HOUR. WALLACE WILL BE HOME BEFORE DINNER.
I'M STANDING THEM BOTH DOWN FOR THE REST OF THE DAY.
CERTAINLY. THEY'VE EARNED IT.

I THINK SO, SIR.

ESTD 1821
THE
LENLIVET
DREET DREET

DREET DRE-
CHACE.
HULLO YOURSELF. YOU *REALLY* SHOULDN'T BE *CALLING* FROM THE *OFFICE*, YOU KNOW *THAT*.

...OH, WELL IF IT'S A *PUB*, THAT'S *DIFFERENT*...
...A *LITTLE*, NOTHING I COULDN'T *HANDLE*...
...ME...?

...I'M JUST WATCHING THE *MATCH*....
GREG RUCKA
LEANDRO FERNANDEZ '07

QUEEN & COUNTRY™

BEHIND THE SCENES

The following pages contain samples of some of Steve Rolston's development process, taking the characters from sketches to final designs, as well as looking at the layout/pencilling process.

Steve's first sketches...

Original designs for Wallace, the Minder who most drastically changed by his final version

OPS ROOM
— 2 feet x 2 feet
8'-wide monitors
16'-wide monitor
8'-wide monitors
trashcan
illuminated glass for viewing map overlays
filing cabinets
Mission Desk
filing cabinets
Men's washroom
phones
Women's washroom
ashtray
Duty Ops Desk
bookcases
slightly raised platform
Horizontal map
photo-copier
hallway
coat rack
chairs
Kitchen
WINDOW
table
T.V. + VCR
water cooler

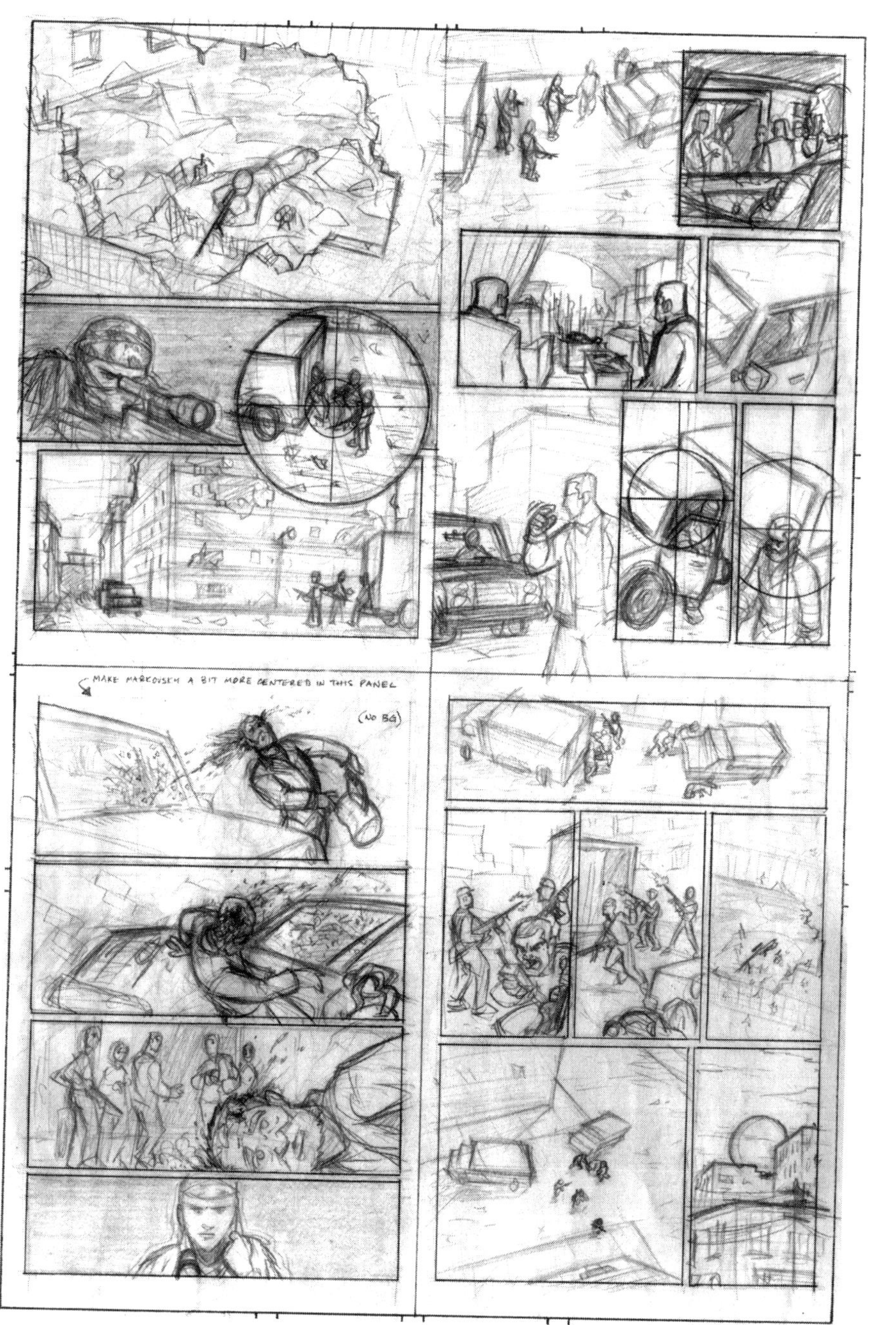

This is an example of how Steve roughed out his pages at a smaller size before he started pencilling them. Figuring out the angles and positioning at this stage allowed him to make changes before starting the detailed work.

What do they mean I'm too cartoony?!

Cartoon by Steve Rolston.

Name's Tara Chace, wot?

Sketch by Bryan O'Malley.

Cartoon by J. Bone.

Cartoons done in response to stuffy critics demanding a more "realistic" style on *Queen & Country.*

PRODUCTION GALLERY

Artist Leandro Fernandez did extensive preparatory work for his tour of duty on Queen & Country. The material is seen here for the first time, and ranges from character sketches and cover designs to a look at his pencilled pages.

PAUL

TARA

Leandro's cover roughs show not only a work in progress, but an assured designer's eye that knew exactly want it wanted to see.

QUEEN &
COUNTRY

QUEEN &
COUNTRY

QUEEN &
COUNTRY

A look at how Leandro maps out his pages.

Note in this sequence from *Operation: Crystal Ball* how the blacks are planned for early on, but left open until the inking.

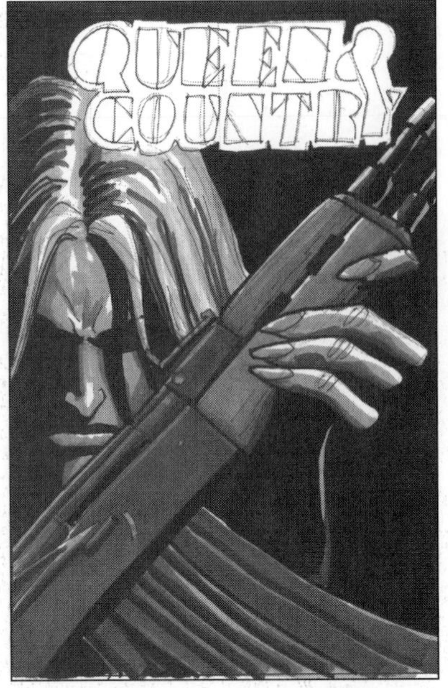

A selection of Leandro's development sketches for the original *Operation: Crystal Ball* trade paperback cover.

QUEEN & COUNTRY

Photos taken at San Diego Comic Con International in 2002, just a couple months after the serialization of *Crystal Ball* began. It is also the convention where Greg Rucka and Steve Rolston won their Eisner Award for *Queen & Country* as Best New Series.

(Right) Behind Leandro and Greg is Greg's wife, Jen Van Meter (*Hopeless Savages*), and she's speaking to Judd Winick (*Pedro & Me*) and his wife, Pam Ling.

(Left) Leandro is flanked by writer Ivan Brandon on the left and one of *Queen & Country's* editors, James Lucas Jones, on the right. You decide which one has already had too many.

QUEEN & COUNTRY™

ABOUT THE AUTHORS . . .

GREG RUCKA was born in San Francisco and raised on the Central Coast of California, in what is commonly referred to as "Steinbeck Country." He began his writing career in earnest at the age of 10 by winning a county-wide short-story contest, and hasn't let up since. He graduated from Vassar College with an A.B. in English, and from the University of Southern California's Master of Professional Writing program with an M.F.A.

He is the author of nearly a dozen novels, six featuring bodyguard Atticus Kodiak, and two featuring Tara Chace, the protagonist of his *Queen & Country* series. Additionally, he has penned several short-stories, countless comics, and the occasional non-fiction essay. In comics, he has had the opportunity to write stories featuring some of the world's best-known characters—Superman, Batman, and Wonder Woman—as well as penning several creator-owned properties himself, such as *Whiteout* and *Queen & Country*, both published by Oni Press. His work has been optioned several times over with *Whiteout*, starring Kate Beckinsale, being the first to actually be made. His servers are also in high demand in a variety of creative fields as a story-doctor and creative consultant.

Greg resides in Portland, Oregon, with his wife, author Jennifer Van Meter, and his two children. He thinks the biggest problem with the world is that people aren't paying enough attention.

STEVE ROLSTON—Steve Rolston is best known as the premiere artist on Greg Rucka's Eisner Award winning spy series *Queen & Country*. Since then he has illustrated *Pounded, Jingle Belle, Mek, Tales of the TMNT, The Escapists* and a forthcoming *DeGrassi* graphic novel. With both his artist and writer hats on, he created the cartoony *Jack Spade & Tony Two-Fist* and the "slacker noir" graphic novel *One Bad Day*.

Steve lives in Vancouver, Canada.

BRIAN HURTT burst onto the comic scene with the second arc in Greg Rucka's critically acclaimed series *Queen & Country*. He's not put his pencil down since, lending his illustration skills to the *Queen & Country* spin-off *Declassified*, *Skinwalker*, DC's critically acclaimed *Gotham Central*, as well as the DC series *Hard Time*. In 2006 he launched a new creator-owned series with writer Cullen Bunn. Titled *The Damned*, the series saw Brian pencil, ink, tone, and letter a book for the first time ever.

He resides just outside of St. Louis in a room covered in black ink.

LEANDRO FERNANDEZ is one of the most versatile and dedicated artist working comics. After taking the industry by storm with his controversial work on *Queen & Country*, he ended up at Marvel Comics and has since worked with some of their most well known characters—including both Wolverine (where he collaborated once again with *Q&C* scribe Greg Rucka) and Spider-Man. He is perhaps best known as the artist of some of Garth Ennis' most powerful *Punisher* stories.

Leandro's work can currently be seen gracing the pages of comics at both Marvel and DC.

BRYAN LEE O'MALLEY—is an award-winning Canadian cartoonist.

His current work (2004 to present) is the *Scott Pilgrim* series, published by Oni Press. His previous efforts include the graphic novel *Lost at Sea* and artwork for the *Hopeless Savages* miniseries *Ground Zero*.

He occasionally records music under the name Kupek.

CHRISTIN NORRIE has worked extensively as an artist since 2000. Her primary work is in comic book illustration, which skills have led to projects creating concept art, storyboards, and book covers.

Her most noted works include her original graphic novel *Cheat* , the Oni Press series *Hopeless Savages*, and the newly released graphic novel *Breaking Up* published in 2007 by Scholastic/Graphix.

Dubbed "a natural storyteller" by *Publisher's Weekly*, Norrie has earned two Eisner nominations, A Russ Manning Promising Newcomer Nomination, and a 9th Panel and New York City Comic Book Museum Award.

She works and lives in New York City.

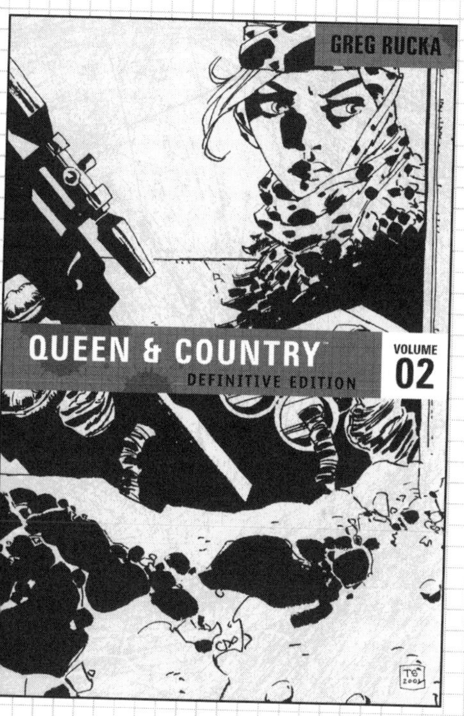

COMING IN 2008 TO FINER COMICS SHOPS & BOOKSTORES.

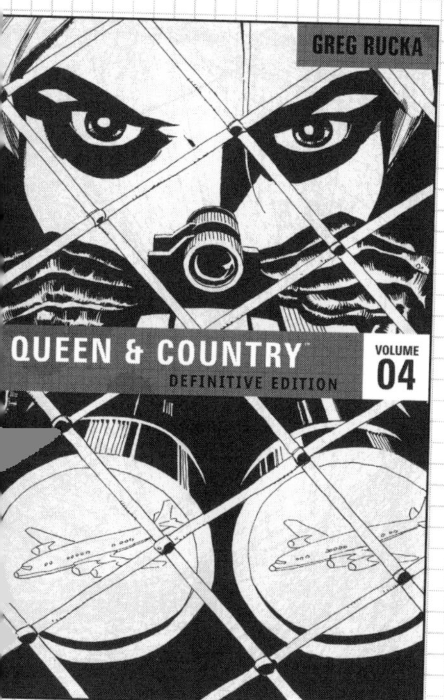

QUEEN & COUNTRY, VOL. 2:
THE DEFINITIVE EDITION
written by Greg Rucka; illustrated by Jason Alexander, Carla Speed McNeil, & Mike Hawthorne
376 pages, 6x9 trade paperback
ISBN-13 978-1-932664-71-3
$19.95 US
COMING APRIL 2008!

QUEEN & COUNTRY, VOL. 3:
THE DEFINITIVE EDITION
written by Greg Rucka; illustrated by Mike Norton, Chris Samnee, & Steve Rolston
296 pages, 6x9 trade paperback
ISBN-13 978-1-932664-96-3
$19.95 US
COMING JULY 2008!

QUEEN & COUNTRY, VOL. 4:
THE DEFINITIVE EDITION
written by Greg Rucka & Antony Johnston; illustrated by Brian Hurtt, Rick Burchett, & Christopher Mitten
296 pages, 6x9 trade paperback
$19.95 US
COMING DECEMBER 2008!